All Powers
Necessary
and Convenient

Act 2, "The Hearings."

All Powers Necessary and Convenient

A play of fact and speculation

Mark F. Jenkins

University of Washington Press

Seattle and London

For my sons, Austin and Noah

Library of Congress Cataloging-in-Publication Data
Jenkins, Mark F.
    All powers necessary and convenient : a play of fact and speculation /
    Mark F. Jenkins. p. cm.
    Includes bibliographical references.
    ISBN 0-295-97939-9 (alk. paper)
    1. Washington (State) Legislature. Joint Legislative Fact-Finding
    Committee on Un-American Activities.—Drama.   2. Anti-communist
    movements—Washington (State)—Seattle—Drama.   3. English
    teachers—Washington (State)—Drama.   4. College teachers—
    Washington (State)—Drama.   5. Seattle (Wash.)—Drama. I. Title.
PS3560.E49A79   2000   99-055768
812'.54—dc21

The guises of power are so various, so dissembled that power ceases to be recognized as such. . . . We delude ourselves. The holders of great power may be physically frail, gentle in manner, tender in sentiment . . . but power is power, and its nature is to grab hold, to seize possession, to overwhelm. Whatever appears in human life that seems unrelated to power, or even—like love, like charity, like self sacrifice—contrary to it, is, if it endures, but another mask of power.

Allen Wheelis, *The Path Not Taken*

He lies like an eyewitness.

A Russian expression

Contents

Foreword

Richard S. Kirkendall

Soon after World War II, a "Red Scare" swept across the United States and became a major part of American culture and politics. Linked with the Cold War in its hostility toward Communists and communism, it also differed from that war. Whereas the American role in the latter focused on the Soviet Union, promoters of the Red Scare expressed alarm about a threat that they located inside the nation. It came, they charged, from Communists in a variety of places, including the U.S. Department of State, the labor unions, the movie industry, the theatre, and the universities. The state of Washington, which had long had a vigorous Left composed of both anticorporate progressives and anticapitalist radicals, supplied one of the early arenas of the Red Scare.

Early in 1998, a person of the theatre, Mark Jenkins, took Seattle people back to that time, a half-century earlier, when their city played a prominent role in the Red Scare. His play, *All Powers Necessary and Convenient,* packed a theatre on University Way for every performance, provoked lively postplay discussions, and stimulated people outside the School of Drama to supplement the theatre experience with a conference, lectures, and other presentations organized under the All Powers Project. Talk about the past and its relevance filled the air. For a historian, as well as many other folks, the occasion was enormously stimulating.

The playwright had thought long, hard, and effectively about ways of bringing the past into the present. Struggling with the tension between art and history—the difficulties in writing something that is both good history and good theatre—he had come up with a creative solution that clearly distinguished fact from speculation. To help his audience see what he was doing and had done, he created a two-part scheme and labeled the various sections of his play either "Theatre of Record" or "Theatre of Conjecture." The first consists of historical sources, including transcripts of legislative hearings, interviews with participants, and newspaper stories. "Theatre of Conjecture" includes some facts—things he knows to be true—but goes beyond them, often well beyond, to portray what might have been said and done in different times and places. Jenkins had done the basic work that historians do; he had explored documents and memories as a means of getting into the past, but in writing his play, he had allowed himself to be more imaginative than historians customarily permit themselves to be.

As the audience saw that February week, Jenkins shifts from one "theatre" to the other throughout his play. Early on, he presents an edited version of a transcript of a legislative hearing, the central event of the play. This is an example of the "Theatre of Record." He is on solid ground here. He has a document that contains all that is said at this point in the play.

Immediately after this episode in document-based history and theatre, Jenkins moves into the "Theatre of Conjecture." The scene is a newspaper office. He knows that a journalist in that office, Fred Niendorff of the *Seattle Post-Intelligencer,* was an active participant in the story, not merely a reporter of it. He collaborated with the central character, Albert Canwell, a first-term legislator from Spokane. These are facts, but the playwright goes beyond them and presents an event that did not occur, at least not just as it appears here. It brings Niendorff and Canwell, real people, together with three fictional characters: a young secretary, a cynical newspaperman, and a tough and ambitious general. During the presentations of the play, alert playgoers did not have to guess whether they were watching fact or fiction. The scene was labeled with the supertitle "Theatre of Conjecture." If they wished, historians among them could turn Jenkins's speculations into hypotheses to be tested. Did an air force officer actually influence the conduct of the hearing in a major way? Did military leaders participate in other episodes of the Red Scare in similar fashion?

The episode raises even more questions. Were the Red Scare, the Cold War, the economy, and the political culture connected with one another as the playwright suggests? Jenkins's general says to Canwell at one point:

> Convincing talk is better than frank talk. I've been doing a fair amount of the latter aimed at a certain, highly placed elected official [the president?]. And I would conclude from all this . . . talk . . . that this high official needs to be convinced that the domestic communist threat from within our borders is . . . *real.* That it is *pervasive.* That it is *dangerous.* The way I see it, *my* job is to convince him that *foreign* communism is an external threat to the U.S., even greater than fascism was. *Your* job is to convince the public that there is a concurrent *internal* threat. A massive threat from those among us American citizens—from within our borders. You reading me?

"I think we understand each other," the legislator replies.

Niendorff carries the subject farther. He wants the general to know "that we here at the *P-I* are also aware of the great potential for an even greater partnership between the new Air Force, the Boeing Company, and the city of Seattle." He suggests that the city is "in the dawn of a new age," but the general interrupts to propose that the politically active journalist is "not gonna see much of a fuckin' dawn as long as this area is regarded as a radical back-water." The journalist promises "to change that perception."

Perhaps nothing like this episode took place. The scene, how-ever, is surely provocative. There are others like it as the play moves forward. They offer suggestions of the kind that historians are, by their nature or training, inclined and equipped to explore. Other folks may also be inspired to look into these matters. The play-wright functioned like a historian in exploring the past; he read original documents, interviewed participants, and shaped hypoth-eses. His play can stimulate historical investigations and provoke historical thought. Theatre and history can interact in these ways.

Nearly all of the characters in the play actually participated in the history with which Jenkins is concerned. He presents carefully drawn sketches of each of them. And the most elaborate portrayal is of Canwell.

This man from Spokane, the play suggests, defined himself as an investigator. "And I want you to know that I have evidence, I have files, I have information—," he says to the general, but the latter is not impressed. Nevertheless, the proud legislator presses on: "All through the thirties and since. The automobile strikes in Detroit—I was *there*. Harry Bridges' waterfront, here in Seattle—I *covered* it. Marx in the libraries—I know who *reads* him." And the general replies: "I know I have a dick between my legs. It's what I do with it that counts." Rather than encourage genuine investigations, he offers Canwell a professional witness who will say under oath whatever they want him to say. Not all promoters of the Red Scare were alike, this exchange implies.

In the play, Canwell appears as an ideologue, genuinely deter-mined to crush the Communists in his state and eager to use his skills and powers as an investigator for this purpose. His ideology has religious and racial dimensions. "Think about it, Al," Niendorff advises as he urges the legislator to use the professional witness.

"When it's all over, you win the door prize. A ticket to higher political office." "That's not why I'm doing this," Canwell responds. "Is that clear? I am a patriot. I happen to believe there is a God looking down on all this." An investigator for many years, he is proud of his work and prefers to rely on his "own information" rather than "an outsider," especially a black man. He also has confidence that he knows what is right and believes he is authorized to impose his convictions on others. They include a young secretary as well as the faculty of the University of Washington. The secretary is a fiction; the faculty members portrayed in the play were real people.

As a strongly ideological person, did Canwell resemble the other participants in the Red Scare? We know that Joseph R. McCarthy, for one, was not an ideologue. In 1948, the junior senator from Wisconsin had not yet become the most prominent representative of the Red Scare mentality. In fact, he would not become a major player until 1950, knew very little about Communists in America, and took up the issue largely to strengthen his position for his reelection campaign in 1952. Al Canwell's anticommunism, on the other hand, was the crusade of a lifetime. The play suggests this was so, and it was.

The investigator's activities in 1948 had roots in his early years, and his anticommunist crusade lasted into his old age. Even as a teenager in Spokane in the 1920s, young Al had begun to learn about the communist presence in his state, and by the 1930s, he had learned more. Working as a journalist in Yakima, he encountered people on the farms he regarded as Communists, and obtaining opportunities to go to Seattle, he witnessed radical activity there. Later in the decade and in the early 1940s, he continued to gather information on the Left, doing so as both a private investigator and a Spokane County deputy sheriff. Often he worked for or with representatives of major corporations, including Idaho mining firms, the Washington Water Power Company, and the Boeing Company. The reputation he acquired as an antiradical investigator provided the basis for his move into the legislature. Impressed by his reputation, a conservative journalist in Spokane, Ashley Holden of the *Spokesman-Review,* persuaded him to run and gave him favorable publicity in 1946. And long after his two-year term in the legislature ended, Canwell continued to play his self-defined role.

The investigator concluded from his experiences that his state was a place of unusually large interest to the international communist movement. Washington housed a number of major strategic facilities, most notably the Grand Coulee Dam, Hanford, and the Boeing plants, and it occupied a crucial place on the route that he believed Soviet invaders would take. Thus, he believed, the Soviets had placed agents throughout Washington State.

To combat the menace he perceived, Canwell joined an informal, nationwide, anticommunist network. It included the Red Squad in the Seattle Police Department, the Immigration and Naturalization Service, the Federal Bureau of Investigation, the Committee on Un-American Activities of the House of Representatives, and comparable legislative bodies in California and other states. From an early point in his career and for many years thereafter, they helped him build a large file on the men and women of the Left. As part of the Hearst Press, the *Seattle Post-Intelligencer* belonged to the network. Niendorff, a prominent reporter for the paper, drafted the legislative resolution that authorized the work of the special committee that Canwell chaired, although he was only a freshman legislator, and gave him close, detailed, and favorable coverage in the pages of the *P-I.*

The menace, as Canwell saw it, was very broad. It was composed of more than members of the Communist Party. It also included a number of individuals and organizations that worked as "fronts" for the Party. The most important and dangerous of these was, in his view, the American Civil Liberties Union.

As a member of the state legislature in 1947–48, Canwell targeted several organizations and individuals, including the Seattle Repertory Playhouse, the Washington State Pension Union, and the University of Washington. Claiming that parents had complained that faculty members had subverted their children, he devoted a week during the summer of 1948 to a public hearing on the university. If he had been reelected that fall, he would have gone farther.

As an investigator both in and out of office, Canwell had a broad, almost unlimited conception of his powers and sought to throw a spotlight on particular individuals. During his years outside the legislature, he vigorously tapped rooms and telephone lines. As chair of Washington State's special committee on un-American activities, he refused to allow lawyers to raise constitutional issues, interrogate witnesses, or do anything but quietly advise their clients. He called upon the people he targeted to testify to their membership in the Communist Party and on the people they had known in it. He did not ask them to tell of their activities as Party members. Instead, he assumed they did what he believed all Communists did, and he turned to other individuals, ex-members of the Party, to testify about the nature of the Communist Party USA. They told him what he already believed to be true: the Soviet Union dominated the Party; it controlled its members, and they engaged in subversive activities.

Canwell placed one highly significant restriction on what he did. He limited himself to investigation and relied upon others to take action against the people he targeted. The play makes this important distinction. "I take fierce pride in the fact that no one and no organization—not even the American Legion—can match the depth and range of my personal investigations of communism in the Pacific Northwest," he advises the general. "I guarantee I will deliver up to you domestic Communists and Party-liners of every stripe and shade. . . . It is up to you fellows on the national scene to take it from there." In Seattle, some key people did what he expected they would do. The patrons of the Repertory Playhouse deserted it, forcing it out of business; the president of the University of Washington, Raymond B. Allen, and the regents, including the labor leader Dave Beck, took action against six veteran and tenured members of the faculty. They fired three of them—Herbert Phillips (Philosophy), Ralph Gundlach (Psychology), and Joseph Butterworth (English)—basically because they were members of the Communist Party, and the three never found academic employment again.

Allen had ambitions for the university. He hoped to take advantage of the state's increased economic strength, largely a product of the wartime development of the Boeing Company, to build the institution into a great national university. He knew that this could not be accomplished without strong public support and assumed that the people of the state would not support the university if they believed there were Communists on the faculty. He also believed that he could not attract talented faculty members if professors around the nation saw the University of Washington as a place that did not respect the principles of academic freedom. So he carved out a new conception of academic freedom that fitted the culture of the Cold War and the Red Scare. He argued that Communists were not free people.

Nearly all that I know about Canwell and the historical episode in which he participated in such a large way I know because of my involvement in the "All Powers Project." I was in Spokane in 1948, an undergraduate at Gonzaga University and aware of Canwell's attack on faculty members on the other side of the Cascades, but I had little understanding of him and his activities. A

half-century later, however, stimulated by the play and my partici-
pation in discussions of it, I read as much as I could about the
events with which the play is concerned and tried to test the hypotheses it offered.

The exchange between Niendorff and the general offers the
most intriguing of the play's hypotheses. It appears in the journalist's
acceptance of a mandate to change the perception of Washington
State as a "radical backwater." What Jenkins proposes here is that
the leading promoters of the Red Scare in the state hoped above
all to change its political culture by destroying the Left. At a later
point, he appears to reinforce this interpretation with an imag-
ined statement by John Caughlan, a lawyer for some of Canwell's
targets. The lawyer maintains that they were involved in a "political struggle," a struggle for *"power."* The "other side" had "reinvented an age-old game in which the main rule is: you are guilty
unless you renounce your thoughts, your beliefs—and the company you keep. They understand the nature and use of power."

This is a political interpretation of the Red Scare, and since
the 1960s, much of the historical scholarship on it has offered just
such an analysis. This way of looking at the phenomenon challenges a psychological version that had emerged during the 1950s
and portrayed it as basically an irrational event, an episode in mass
hysteria. The newer view emphasizes rational calculations made
by politicians, both Democrats and Republicans, to serve their
own interests. Democrats employed the themes in hope of main-
taining their party in power against challenges from both Henry
A. Wallace's Progressive Party and the Republicans. The latter used
Red Scare themes as a means of returning their party to the domi-
nant position it had occupied for a generation before the Great
Depression of the 1930s. Now, Mark Jenkins, with his suggestion
that Canwell and his allies sought to change the political culture,
offers a version of the political interpretation that fits the special

circumstances of the state of Washington. It was a place in which anticorporate progressives and anticapitalist radicals had at times possessed substantial political strength.

Since the end of the Cold War, an interpretation has emerged that presents many Red Scare activists more favorably than the earlier interpretations did. Drawing upon new information that became available after the collapse of the Soviet Union and the opening of Soviet archives, the latest version suggests that these activists often had good reasons for what they did, for some American Communists seriously betrayed the United States. "We now know," Sam Tanenhaus wrote in *The New York Review* (January 14, 1999), "that the American Communist Party served from its inception in 1919 as an outpost of the Moscow-based Communist International . . . and that a disciplined espionage 'apparatus,' controlled by Soviet intelligence, infiltrated the US government in the 1930s and 1940s and placed spies inside the Manhattan Project at Los Alamos."

The new evidence does not challenge our playwright's story. Canwell, his allies on the committee, the friendly witnesses that appeared before it, and the university authorities did not offer evidence that the professors who would lose their academic careers were controlled by Moscow, engaged in acts of espionage, or made plans to do so. Furthermore, the hearings on and off campus did not demonstrate that the professors used their classrooms to indoctrinate their students. In addition, the post–Cold War scholarship has not revealed that these professors were Soviet espionage agents. In fact, they are not mentioned in the major works. They do not appear in Richard Gid Powers's *Not without Honor: The History of American Anti-communism* (1995). They cannot be found in the recent books by Harvey Klehr, John Earl Haynes, and Fridrikh Igorevich Firsov: *The Secret World of American Communism* (1995) and *The Soviet World of American Commu-*

nism (1998). They are not players in the story told by Allen Weinstein and Alexander Vassiliev in *The Haunted Wood: Soviet Espionage in America—The Stalin Era* (1999). They did not deserve to be purged from a university faculty.

Mark Jenkins offers many insights into and a large interpretation of the Albert Canwell story, an important part of the history of Washington State. In doing so, he demonstrates that theatre and history can collaborate successfully. He has explored the past and relied heavily on historical documents to advance his story but has not stopped there. He has also moved beyond the documents and employed the imagination of a playwright to develop the tale in some of the most significant and provocative ways. All along, by the use of supertitles, he has alerted his audience to what he is doing, encouraging them to deal critically with the play and explore the subject on their own. If they wish, historians can test his boldest ideas. By implication, he challenges them to do so.

Preface

Historical Basis of the Play

In 1948 two public hearings occurred in Seattle, the ostensible purpose of which was to investigate individuals and organizations "whose activities are such as to undermine the stability of our American institutions: confuse and mislead the people." The enabling resolution went on to proclaim that "subversive persons and groups are endangering our domestic unity . . . and under cover of the protection afforded by the Bill of Rights these persons and groups seek to destroy our liberties and our freedom . . . and to subject us to the domination of foreign power." Those who advocated, organized, and ran the hearings were to "exercise all powers necessary or convenient to accomplish the objects and purposes . . . " etc.[1]

These hearings were conceived of and set in motion by the Washington State Legislature. The Joint Legislative Fact-Finding Committee on Un-American Activities in the State of Washington, as it was officially named, became popularly known as the Canwell Committee, after its leader, freshman representative from Spokane, Albert Canwell. What happened in Seattle was an early and potent tryout for what was soon to become, on a national level, the McCarthy era. The committee subpoenaed documents and witnesses. Uncooperative witnesses, most of whom were professors at the University of Washington, were charged with contempt and some were fined and sent to jail. Three tenured profes-

1. House Concurrent Resolution no. 10, Washington State Legislature, 1948.

sors were fired from the university, and three others were put on probation, never to receive further advancement in rank or salary. Even people at the university who were not called before the committee found their reputations suspect and their careers stifled for being friends or close colleagues of those who were. A local theatre company with a distinguished national reputation and loosely associated with the university, the Seattle Repertory Playhouse (no relationship to the current Seattle Repertory Theatre), was also targeted. As a result of the hearings, the theatre company lost its audience support and was forced out of existence. A political chill, sometimes escalating into fever, spread through the university, the city, the state, and the region. The crisis eventually joined and fed into a national mood that generated powerful "anticommunist" actions that lasted well into the 1960s. Aftershocks of damage done to dissenting U.S. citizens during the early Cold War period, especially within the families of the affected, are still felt today.

These were hearings, not trials. Trials came later. It was not against the law to be a member of the Communist Party. It is important to remember that the usual rules and procedures of a court of law did not apply. Most notably there was no right of cross-examination, no strict rules of evidence, and no resolution for those who were accused of communist sympathies. Again, the purpose of the hearings was to expose groups and individuals thought to be Communists, or "Liberals" thought to be communist sympathizers or "fellow travelers." Among the creeds put forth by the committee was that "a man is known by the company he keeps." That translated into the principle of guilt by association.

The hearings did not take place in a vacuum. The "Left," including its most organized manifestation, the Communist Party USA, was a notable force during the depression. Washington State boasted a large and effective "progressive" movement. World War II had recently ended. The United States had dropped two atom bombs on Japan. Churchill had just given his now famous talk in Fulton, Missouri, declaring an "iron curtain" had fallen across Europe. Stalin was not getting good press; his ruthlessness was becoming known. Having dropped two atomic weapons, there was widespread fear in the country of what might happen if Russia got the bomb. Even though membership in the Communist Party USA had decreased from a high of about 300,000 in the 1930s down to roughly a third of that by the end of the war, a kind of mass fear was developing in this country, and certain people leveraged that fear into an even greater hysteria. According to ex–deputy sheriff and self-styled investigator Albert Canwell, the state of Washington was "acrawl with trained and iron disciplined Communists . . . softening up our people" as a prelude to a land and sea invasion originating in Siberia, moving across Alaska, and then snaking its way into the Puget Sound region, where the Boeing Company and other nationally sensitive operations were waiting like sitting ducks.[2] On a national level, a propaganda machine was gearing up with the help of J. Edgar Hoover of the FBI, newspaper magnate William Randolph Hearst, gossip columnist Walter Winchell, and much of the Hollywood establishment.

Indeed, there were a few members, and former members, of the Communist Party USA on the faculty of the University of Washington. There were others who were left-leaning liberals active in civic and state politics who in time fell under suspicion as fellow travelers. Canwell has said, "We have the right and responsibility to preserve the system. And if we have to step on a few toes to do it, so be it."[3]

2. Joint Legislative Fact-Finding Committee on Un-American Activities, *Un-American Activities in Washington State: Report to the 31st Washington Legislature* (Olympia, 1949), pp. 1, 4.

3. *Albert F. Canwell: An Oral History,* Washington State Oral History Program (Olympia: Office of the Secretary of State, 1997), p. 294.

Once the investigations began, the rules of this game were as follows: If called before the committee, the implication was that you were either a "Red," a former Red, or a fellow traveler and, by implication, a traitor. Once targeted, your only recourse, and proof of patriotism, was a public confession. Further, in order to reinforce your remorse, you were required to name anyone else you knew to be, or thought to be, a Communist, be that person friend, family, or associate.

The responses of the subpoenaed witnesses can be broken down into several categories:

those who would not cooperate with the committee in any substantial way and in various ways defied it (among these were those who lost their jobs and were charged with contempt), those who admitted past Communist Party membership but would not name others,

those who feigned ignorance or lack of memory,

those who named names under duress,

those who were eager to name names ("friendly" witnesses), and

those who committed perjury by inventing damaging testimony about others.

In the months and weeks prior to the hearings, both the *Seattle Times* and the Hearst-owned *Seattle Post-Intelligencer* published stories on communism, averaging one every other day. Fred Niendorff, business editor of the *Post-Intelligencer*, actually helped Canwell write the legislation that enabled the committee to come into existence. Niendorff played a crucial behind-the-scenes role for the committee. He wrote stories during the hearings distorting and sensationalizing the already outrageous claims made by the committee and its witnesses. The hearings were an inquisition and an early and effective example of a growing mood in this country, at midcentury, of rabid intolerance for unsanctioned thought.

One further note of context: The American West in general and Washington State to a concentrated degree, from their earliest days as territories, attracted people with distinctly differing attitudes and beliefs. There were those who might be described as pioneers, "rugged individualists," people starting their lives anew, some God fearing, and often suspicious of issues that didn't offer practical solutions. I grew up in such an environment in Wyoming. However, in contrast to Wyoming, the extreme Northwest, from its earliest territorial days, has also been a magnet for those who could be described as freethinking and anti-Puritan. Many nonconforming, experimental communities, founded on nontraditional spiritual beliefs, socially utopian principles, even "free-love" communes and communities, are part of Washington State's early heritage. A third strain of early Washingtonians were those who engaged in radical labor activities in the forests, on the waterfronts, and in industry. This Northwest has continuously experienced, in a variety of ways, a noticeable degree of polarization and consequent friction between eastern and western Washington, between labor and industry, between the less educated and the intelligentsia, between the devout and the secular, between rural and urban. From these populations come the players in this drama.

But even so, the main questions that fueled me were: Why did this event happen? What allows such injustices and fears to germinate, grow, and flourish—and to do so much damage? What does it imply that state legislators could actually pass an enabling law allowing "all powers necessary or convenient" (a fascistic expedient) to lubricate an investigation of its citizens. Wouldn't any student of the Constitution see such means as an abomination of its basic principles? (The Washington State Supreme Court upheld the committee's right to hold and conduct these hearings in the manner it did.) The U.S. Supreme Court upheld the right to conduct such hearings on a national scale. This level of hysteria and determination by some of our citizens to demonize other citizens intrigued and frightened me. It still does. As I write this during the Clinton impeachment, I am again struck by my political naivete.

After all the people I have met and spoken to, after all the reading and research, after all my effort in developing this work, the shortest answer I can give to these questions—and it is not really an answer at all but a meditation—is my play.

A Note on the Form

All Powers Necessary and Convenient is a combination of fact and fiction: some of the scenes derive from verbatim testimony and quotes from newspapers and personal interviews, and some I have completely made up. The play therefore falls under the general category of fiction. One can debate how "factual" any statement is when selected, edited, depicted, and put into altered contexts. One can also debate the preeminence of fiction to expose essential truths, the kind of truth which literal truth often precludes. Nonetheless, I think it is important for the reader to be aware of a definite and deliberate distinction I make between sources of record and sources imaginative.

The Artistic Basis of the Play

One of the theatre's duties, besides telling a good story, is to provide intellectual, emotional, and sensory stimulation giving each audience member the opportunity to experience an altered perspective. Theatre is supposed to help us come to terms with our existence and, at the same time, to alert us as to how we fit into our own sense of "community." Certain theatre experiences can reveal and challenge both our personal and our social needs. When done well, theatre invites the audience to receive this stimulation and perspective experientially, *vicariously,* in a kind of waking dream. Plays are live events that occur in real time and space. This gives them a potential "charge" of immediacy that no other medium offers. We receive the play in the company of other audience members, who temporarily join together—as private souls and, at the same time, as public citizens. A theatre experience can be hallowed. It can become a ritual, a ceremony, and sometimes it can create "myth"—while we are watching, hearing, absorbing. This is theatre's basic function: secular but of the spirit.

The Process

I was drawn to the material of this play, in part, because it records a heated crisis that seared its participants (and some of its observers) in the most public and private ways. The crisis interested me and I thought it important.

However, I don't think I could have forged this play into being without some particular and personal drive within me, part altruistic and part mischievous. My fervor grew as I wrote and reworked the play. I began, not with an ambition to write plays, but simply by taking a first step in response—a deep affective response—to my reading of two volumes of decades-old testimony that I happened to stumble upon at a friend's cabin more than ten years ago.

In retrospect, I believe the most authentic ingredients in the process of writing this play are that I embraced two qualities I would not consciously aspire to: naivete and grandiosity. I now also realize that these two qualities are probably essential for creativity.

My first reading of the transcripts entitled *Un-American Activities in Washington State, 1948,* drew me into the center of a crisis, one that I found intriguing, disturbing, and complicated—delicious issues for the theatre. As an actor I am conditioned to be able to read dialogue and visualize the scene. The transcripts trembled with life, though much of it inferred. There were heroes of a kind and scoundrels and, more interestingly, those who were neither. There were acts of brutality and moments of grace; almost every action was fragmented, interrupted. From what I read, much was implied. There were incidents of struggle and defeat. There seemed to be no real victories, only damage. And for what? What was gained? In a few instances there were triumphs of sorts, triumphs, at least, of the spirit.

I was acquainted with other issues of "un-American activities," having worked as an actor in New York and Hollywood during the 1960s and 1970s. I knew several people who had been blacklisted, both writers and actors. My first professional acting jobs were with the great Joseph Papp, head of the New York Shakespeare Festival, who had been blacklisted out of television in the 1950s. On various occasions I met and talked with Dalton Trumbo, one of the Hollywood Ten, and fellow blacklisted writers Walter Bernstein and Waldo Salt. Each of them had impressed me enormously for their common qualities of undaunted grit and courage. In the late 1960s, my agent, Jack Fields, was, on the side, an effective and committed political activist and altruist (an odd mixture in a Hollywood agent, let me assure you). He was determined to help many blacklisted actors land their first Hollywood jobs in, for some, as many as twenty years. I met several of these people. Among these were the cheerful and lively as well as the broken, sad, and bitter. I saw secondhand how the blacklist worked and the awful toll it took. I also saw the discomfort of the television and motion picture industry in having these artists swept back out from under the rug.

I did not hear of the 1948 Washington State hearings until a few years after I left Hollywood for Seattle. The title *Un-American Activities in Washington State* seemed to jump off the shelf of my friend's cabin and into my field of vision. I sat down and opened one of the volumes to a random page. I knew right away this was for me. I borrowed both volumes and read all the nearly thousand pages within the next couple of days. The subject matter and the specific playing out of the hearings bore into me. Sensing the potential, I set out to try to make a play out of the incidents of the second volume of hearings. I had seen William Devane's production of Eric Bentley's *Are You Now, or Have You Ever Been?* in Hollywood. At Seattle's Empty Space Theatre, I had acted in Emily Mann's *Still Life*, a powerful docudrama. Theatre that was wrought from documentation interested me. I hoped there was a play embedded in the transcripts and that I would be able to distill the hearings into a theatrically viable script. I reduced the second hearing's 400 pages (representing five days' worth of testimony) down to what seemed like a manageably sized script. I then convinced about twenty actor friends to donate an evening of their time to read my material aloud. The reading confirmed that the basic material had exciting episodes, was riddled with ironies and injustices, and contained a variety of compelling conflicts. However, it was not a play. It was a series of fragments—glimpses only. I also learned, neophyte that I was, that 150 pages of dialogue can take about three and a half hours to read. Barry Witham and Betty Comtios, at the University of Washington, read the script and urged me to "go back into the material" and make a play out of it. I was encouraged and discouraged in about equal measure. Since I was an actor, not a writer, I didn't feel I had the skills to do what was needed to make it become a play. It was just too daunting. I had other responsibilities. I put it away. For several years.

In the meantime my work in the theatre began to branch out from acting into directing and teaching. I began to work a step removed from the powerful but subjective angle of the actor. My perspective of what goes on in theatre expanded like a lens moving to wide angle. I eventually helped found Freehold Theatre Lab Studio in Seattle, an organization devoted in part to supporting and encouraging development of new works. Eventually I reread the manuscript. Now I saw its potential with different eyes. Again, I was drawn into the dramas and to the people in those dramas. Once more, I was struck with how clearly the hearings, like any witch-hunt, became a crucible for those who were forced to be involved. Characters in great crisis are the electrons of the theatre. I still found the inherent conflicts tantalizing. I sensed the mischief making that writing affords to the writer. I experienced grandiosity. "What if I could make this work?" I asked myself. The basic material still seemed to be provocative. It takes place at the center of a historically important political and sociological event. Since most people my age or younger had never heard of the Canwell hearings I was beginning to feel a responsibility to try to tell this story and make it work for the theatre. I committed to doing a rewrite and presenting a staged reading of it at Freehold.

I envisioned a more informed, fleshed-out docudrama. I would supply context and perspective. I began reading everything I could get my hands on about the hearings, including accounts from members of the Communist Party who had lived through those times. I perused old newspaper accounts about other hearings and about the McCarthy era in general. I began tracking down surviving witnesses and other participants. I recruited a friend with video equipment to record interviews. I made arrangements to talk with people who had been involved with the hearings, including John Caughlan, attorney for several of the "unfriendly" witnesses. Through a friend I was able to locate Albert Canwell's phone number in Spokane. I called him and he agreed to an interview. I flew to Spokane with my videographer and we heard his version of the investigation and hearings. I interviewed Ted Astley and E. Harold Eby, both unfriendly witnesses, who have since died. The families of some of the deceased witnesses gave me personal papers and copies of FBI transcripts. Nearly everyone I approached was co-operative and wanted their story told.

I faced a new issue. I was both acquiring a new order of magnitude of raw material and trying to compress the material in order to make a shorter script. I wrote and rewrote; I added and subtracted. I reduced the actual testimony further. The process resulted in a new script that included my new, surrounding material. I gathered generous actors again. As I worked on staging it, I was struck with the enthusiasm the actors had for the material, for the subject matter. Several of the actors told me they liked dealing with "socially relevant" material. The staged reading at Freehold revealed that what I had come up with was clearly more interesting, more significant, but, alas, not yet a play—and it was still over three hours long.

But the reading left no doubt that a powerful piece of theatre was embedded in the work I had done up to this point. I became convinced I could and would dig it out. I had a growing sense that if I could bring it off, the play would have not only a theatrical impact but a civic impact. If I could craft a workable play, a terrific, communal encounter with the past might result. This promise appealed to me greatly. My ambition became greater than my doubts about myself as a writer.

Something else began to take place as well. I found myself sliding into the sensibility an actor experiences when creating a role. I was noticing that I had begun to identify with the characters. That is, I was beginning to see the world from their points of view as I focused on each of them. (As part of the process of creating a role, an actor, like a lawyer, first becomes an advocate for whomever he or she plays; otherwise, the "creative leap" into a new, conditional reality cannot take place.) I began to "see" through some of the characters' eyes. I "felt" their lives, both within and outside the context of the hearings. I knew that in order for theatre to take place, an audience would need to experience these things too. This desire served as the catalyst for the next stage of my work. Since the transcripts are simply a record of the words of people whose feet were, so to speak, put to the fire, I realized I would have to re-create the fire. I would have to see and perhaps even smell the burning. What was driving me was not altruism but something else: fascination with the vicarious experience of the struggles.

Another part of me became plagued with more general questions: What was the nature of the fear, the compulsion to conform, the intolerance of unsanctioned thought, in a nation built on principles of that which is not sanctioned? What did the new, Cold War world look like to middle-class America (those who, at least tacitly, endorsed the witch-hunts)? What drove someone to become a Communist, to join and then to stay with the Party after learning of Stalin's Terror? And, how could the supposedly enlightened, educated, self-described liberal-minded, in positions of power and influence, so consistently buckle under to the nascent totalitarianism the Red Scare was igniting in America? How did Canwell truly justify his wanton destruction of so many lives and reputations?

Not having directly experienced these times and issues, I was challenged to guess, to speculate. I became interested in the strain in the American (or human) psyche that is afraid of its own shadow. One question was, what is the nature of playing out private, hidden compulsions in matters of great and public consequence? In order to accurately explain my process, however, I must reverse the question: What do public acts of brutality imply about the private, hidden compulsions of the perpetrator? I reread parts of *Moby Dick*.

Other questions arose. The transcripts and most contemporary accounts only obliquely address what it was like behind the scenes before, during, and after the hearings. I was aware that such issues are not to be approached cognitively so much as presented, or *displayed,* in the situations and behaviors, in the re-creation of the chaos of the moments, *in the moments,* as they happened and as they *might have happened.* I knew that I had to lead the audience, in the safety of its numbers and the promise of a final curtain, to experience the various personal crises brought about by the confluence and collisions of these actual events.

The raw material itself has a kind of epic sweep, involving many characters and stories. I wanted the hearings to be seen to affect a variety of people, not just a few. I made a major commitment about the form of the play. I decided there would be many characters, each of whom would tell only part of the story. That would take care of the sweep. But what about intimacy?

Intimacy—the scope of the events could be of value only if it was a backdrop to personal crisis. I changed course. The documentary form became insufficient for my evolving vision of the play. I isolated myself in a cabin (near where I had come across the transcripts years before) and, miles from any distractions, began to write scenes of fiction, scenes of metaphor, scenes of speculation. I had not realized to what extent I had absorbed, had internalized these characters. I had no idea the extent to which I had assimilated my research. This stage of the writing was an outpouring. As I wrote, I began to taste a character's fear or, in another, revel in political power, righteousness, and unexplainable but authentic compulsions. I experienced outrage on my skin, felt the ache of betrayal in my chest. I experienced the eroticism of power. This influx of sensations was familiar to me as an actor. But I was experiencing more than one role. While writing, I became each character. These characters struggled, grappled, suffered, fought, and spoke. It seems in large part I just wrote down what they said. But it was also physical work. I stood up, paced, sat down, wrote, paced again, tried to maintain and control what I can only describe as a weird kinesthetic, all-encompassing endeavor of something like— delivery. This process took several weeks. It remains one of the most intense and full experiences of my creative life.

My next task was to interweave the new fictional scenes with scenes from the record. This third draft, even when heavily re-worked and edited, resulted in a rather large (and heavy) manu-script of over 200 pages—perhaps three times the length of a nor-mal script. Now what?

Freehold again provided a most useful forum. I was able to gather wonderful and generous actors for yet another staged read-ing. Over a period of several weeks we rehearsed. I edited and rewrote constantly. The rehearsals were charged with enthusiasm and insight from the actors. I had recruited a combination of sea-soned pros as well as less experienced Freehold students as actors. I noticed that Freehold students who were not directly involved in the reading began volunteering, wanting to help. Others began hanging around the rehearsals to see what was going on.

When it was time to present this reading to invited audiences, the playing time was something approaching a staggering seven hours! A little long, these days, for an evening of theatre. We pre-sented half of the script each evening, over four evenings, result-ing in two full showings (and hearings) of the script. Between each reading I made cuts so I could see the effects at the next reading. We held discussions with the audiences after each presen-tation.

What did I learn besides that it was impossibly long? It not only had sweep, it had sprawl. It was all over the place. (I would wager nothing can encourage a playwright to be merciless with his or her work than to have it read by good actors with an audience in attendance.) It also became clear that many of the scenes worked very well and that some of the compelling aspects of this story were actually emerging. The audiences were excited, charged up, and frank in what they had to say about the material. I was surprised that virtually no one, including some people who had been directly involved in the Canwell hearings, objected to my mixing of fact and fiction.

I should say I never seriously considered turning the entire play into fiction. I would make this a play of both fact and speculation, record and conjecture. Why did I need both? The record itself, it had become obvious, could not address all the issues I wanted to present; it could not explore character beyond the hearing rooms. Then why not chuck out the nonfiction as such and call it fiction, change the names and get on with it? For two reasons. First, I was convinced that if I included some of the actual (or close to actual) dialogue as well as actual events under the rubric of "fiction," an audience would question whether such things could have occurred the way they did. Second, I anticipated there would be an inherent dramatic charge in re-creating outrageous actuality. By deciding to intersperse these two kinds of scenes, I immediately faced two challenges: the challenge of verisimilitude and the challenge of style. Would the scenes I made up be convincing next to actual testimony dialogue? And even if I was able to achieve a sense of authenticity, would the two kinds of scenes dovetail stylistically with one another?

With these issues facing me I began the fourth version. I slashed, I cut, I reworked scenes, even wrote new scenes, and threw away page after page after page. During this phase of the work I began the daunting task of addressing dramatic structure: architecture, economy, cause and effect. For the next year and a half, I grappled with these issues of craft so as to bring this material into a form that would do the story justice.

The Production

The premier production at the University of Washington's Playhouse Theatre ran just under four hours. The entire run of the initial production sold out weeks in advance. An added performance sold out in one day. Every performance received a standing ovation. The reviews were excellent. Some audience members were reluctant to leave the performance until they were able to talk to someone about it.

In many ways the Playhouse, adjacent to the main University of Washington campus, was an ideal venue for the production since the building itself is one of the locales in the play. The building was conceived of, financed, constructed, and used by the Seattle Repertory Playhouse until the university, after the hearings, in a rather shady deal, acquired the building, having taken advantage of the Canwell episode. Ironies abound. By presenting the play in the building, the sense of history was alive and palpable for the audience as well as for the actors who rehearsed and played in it. For years the building was burdened with the name the Glenn Hughes Playhouse, honoring the former head of the School of Drama who betrayed the original company members to help expedite the university's acquisition of the theatre. In 1993, Barry Witham, former head of the university's School of Drama, had Hughes's name removed from his "conquest." The Glenn Hughes Playhouse became the Playhouse Theatre. In addition, as part of my agreement to do the play at the university, I asked that a permanent plaque be installed honoring the artistic work of the Seattle Repertory Playhouse from 1929 to 1951. The plaque also makes reference to the hearings as a factor in the disintegration of the company. It was unveiled after the last performance. I hope some ghosts were laid to rest.

In the month before the opening of the show, various departments of the university presented speakers, forums, colloquia, displays, and a Web page all under the title "The All Powers Project" in order to address the history of the hearings, their context, and implications for today.

The final performance was dedicated to surviving witnesses, their friends and families. Several people traveled hundreds of miles to attend. Following the performance people in the audience were invited to speak of their own experiences. They did. Another kind of theatre, a theatre of testament, came to be for a few hours. People spoke from deep experience. Some spoke of old pain, but pain that had defined lives that followed the lives of those I depicted in my play. People spoke of their parents' courage and suffering in ways that made me understand that their traumas and the traumas of their families had evolved over time into a kind of myth. Such is another function of theatre: to create myth from actual experience. I felt a profound sense of completion that last day of the life of the original production of my play.

Before this publication, I edited several more scenes that, during production, revealed themselves to be making redundant points. I cut other scenes that were so specific to the history of the University of Washington as to make them irrelevant to a wider public.

Tip O'Neill said, "All politics is local." Indeed, the politics surrounding the events of 1948 were, at first, local in nature. A few years later they became national, and even international, and were given the label "McCarthyism." Then, fifty years later, the mythological reincarnation of the events became, once again, a local political, civic, historic event of another kind, made so by means of a local theatrical effort. The "local" issues revealed in the events of half a century ago are, I believe, extreme manifestations of ongoing tensions within human nature and, in specific ways, reflect the nature of American culture. Continuing in O'Neill's vein one could say that all actions are, at first, *personal.* But it works both ways. If politics is local, the results sometimes are not. They can cover vast territory. By the same token, all actions no matter how personal, to quote John Caughlan in a scene from the play, are also *political.* This was my main discovery in the writing of this play.

Mark F. Jenkins
Seattle, Washington
February 1999

Acknowledgments

The collaborative nature of theatre is such that, except for the solitude of writing, nothing happens without other people's skills, talents, and great goodwill. Most especially, I owe a debt of gratitude to Sarah Nash Gates for her encouragement and fierce championing of my script, for her determination to bring it first to life at the University of Washington, and for her elegant vision of the All Powers Project. I am also grateful for her enthusiasm and her abilities in garnering broad support for the production.

I thank my director, Victor Pappas, for his insights, vision, and execution of a production that, due to his talents, stirred the uninitiated as well as those whose lives were seared by the hearings. I am deeply indebted to Jane Phillips, daughter of Professor Herbert J. Phillips, for giving me access to his personal papers and FBI file; to Guy and Maia Astley for turning over to me virtually all Ted Astley's papers and files; to the late John Caughlan for sharing his experiences and for his incisive analysis of communism in America; to Murray and Rosa Morgan for their perspectives; to Wilmot Ragsdale, whose volumes of the hearing transcripts sparked my efforts. I thank those who contributed time, talent, and equipment for videotaping: David Churchill, Kirk Arndt, Western Video Services, and Patti Rosendahl.

I owe a special thanks to Wayne Martin, who, with no previous experience in the theatre, faced the many challenges and varied tasks of "project manager" with great effectiveness.

I thank the members of the All Powers Project Steering Committee for shepherding good ideas into concrete civic events. I especially thank Len Schroeter, legendary civil rights lawyer, and Pat Soden, director of the University of Washington Press, for their early and crucial interest in the potential of the play. I'm grateful to Margaret Levi, holder of the Harry Bridges Chair at the Center for Labor Studies at the University of Washington, for her support and for serving as a moderator for several discussions of the play. Others who made the project larger than the play itself were historian Richard Kirkendall, facilitator Diane Robbins, and librarians Linda Gould and Karyl Wynn. For her kind support and counsel, I thank Kate Hendricks.

I am most grateful to the eighty-four individuals and organizations whose generous financial support made the production possible. I thank the faculty and staff of the University of Washington's School of Drama for supporting the extra and, sometimes, inconvenient demands made by the production of the play. I am very grateful to Nicole Boyer-Cochran for typing the script and its many revisions during rehearsals; to Janet Nicholas and Dan Morris for their research and copying of newspaper articles; and to my editor, Pamela Bruton, of the University of Washington Press, for her sharp eye for detail and for her insightful suggestions.

Finally, I hold dear the support, patience, and most generous love of Carol Mason, who lends light and grace to my life and my efforts.

All Powers
Necessary
and Convenient

Characters

ALBERT CANWELL, chairman of the Joint Legislative Fact-Finding Committee on Un-American Activities in the State of Washington in 1948

AMERICAN CIVIL LIBERTIES UNION (ACLU) ATTORNEY

JOSEPH BUTTERWORTH, professor of English, University of Washington, target of committee

SENATOR THOMAS BIENZ, member of committee

WILLIAM HOUSTON, chief investigator of committee

JOHN CAUGHLAN, attorney for several subpoenaed witnesses

DEMONSTRATOR

FRED NIENDORFF, business editor for the *Seattle Post-Intelligencer*

VIOLA JAEGER, editorial assistant at the *Seattle Post-Intelligencer*, later secretary to the committee

CONRAD CURLEW, columnist for the *Seattle Post-Intelligencer*

GENERAL WALTER J. ASHLEY, member of U.S. Joint Chiefs of Staff

JOEY BUTTERWORTH, mentally retarded son of Joe Butterworth

MAUD BEAL, professor of English, University of Washington, target of committee

MORROW JEWELL, private detective, consultant to the committee

ANGELO PELLEGRINI, professor of English, target of committee

MELVIN RADER, professor of philosophy, target of committee

GEORGE HEWITT, professional witness for the committee

ALETHIA HEWITT, wife of George Hewitt

MRS. FLORENCE BEAN JAMES, codirector of Seattle Repertory Playhouse, target of committee

ALBERT OTTENHEIMER, codirector and actor, Seattle Repertory Playhouse, target of committee

STAGE MANAGER, Seattle Repertory Playhouse

HERBERT J. (SCOOP) PHILLIPS, professor of philosophy, target of committee

J. EDGAR HOOVER, director, Federal Bureau of Investigation

BRENT STIRLING, professor of English

RAYMOND B. ALLEN, president of the University of Washington, 1946–51

SOPHUS KEITH WINTHER, head of English Department, friendly witness to the committee

HELGA PHILLIPS, wife of "Scoop" Phillips, target of committee

TED ASTLEY, vocation counselor, University of Washington, target of committee

RALPH GUNDLACH, professor of psychology, target of committee

MELVILLE JACOBS, professor of anthropology, target of committee

E. HAROLD EBY, professor of English, target of committee

GARLAND ETHEL, professor of English, target of committee

BURTON JAMES, codirector, Seattle Repertory Playhouse, target of committee

CLIFFORD O'BRIEN, attorney for several subpoenaed witnesses

C. T. HATTEN, attorney for Joseph Butterworth

ED HENRY, attorney for several subpoenaed witnesses

DAVE BECK, president of the Teamsters Union, member of University of Washington Board of Regents

MRS. DABNEY, Social Services worker

AARON J. LEVY, judge, state of New York

MARSINAH CANWELL, wife of Albert Canwell

COURT OFFICIALS, STATE PATROLMEN, MILITARY ESCORTS, REPORTERS, PHOTOGRAPHERS

Place

Committee hearing room and various other locations around the city of Seattle, the state of Washington, and the United States.

Time

Between 1948 and 1998.

LOBBY PRELUDE

The lobby of the theatre may be part of the production, displaying newspaper photos, clippings from the 1948 hearings, and contextual information. A time line covering major leftist events from the time of Marx to the present day might be included.

At fifteen minutes before curtain some of the actors mingle with the audience and, choosing nine or ten members of the soon-to-be audience, ask each to accept a piece of paper with a name written on it, these being the names of subpoenaed witnesses who will be identified only once. These volunteer audience members will be asked to stand briefly when that name is called as the hearing section of the play gets under way. The proxy witnesses, along with the actors portraying the rest of those called, will be set upon by "newspaper photographers" when they stand.

Act 1, "The Visit": René Millán (Houston) and Tom Spiller (Butterworth).

ACT ONE

The audience enters a dimmed hearing room setting. Projected on a screen to one side is a reproduction of the green cover of the 1848 edition of the Communist Manifesto. *On a screen, center, paragraphs of the* Manifesto *are projected:*

EUROPE 1848

There is a specter haunting Europe—the specter of Communism. All the powers of old Europe have entered into a holy alliance to exorcize this specter: Pope and Czar, Metternich and Guizot, French radicals and German police-spies. . . . Communists everywhere support every revolutionary movement against the existing social and political order of things. . . .

. . . Our epoch, the epoch of the bourgeoisie, possesses, however, this distinctive feature: it has simplified the class antagonisms. Society as a whole is more and more splitting up into two great hostile camps, into two great classes directly facing each other: bourgeoisie and proletariat. . . .

. . . The Communists disdain to conceal their views and aims. They openly declare that their ends can be attained only by the forcible overthrow of all existing social conditions.

Let the ruling classes tremble at the Communistic revolution.

The proletarians have nothing to lose but their chains.

They have a world to win.

WORKING MEN OF ALL COUNTRIES, UNITE!

As the audience is seated, three men enter downstage of the hearing room in separate pools of light facing the audience: ALBERT CANWELL, *elderly and casual;* JOSEPH BUTTERWORTH, *aged and disheveled; and a retired* ACLU ATTORNEY, *vital, in his seventies. They speak directly to the audience.*

CANWELL: I'm always surprised, the various interests in my activities. They're fifty years in the past. They should be forgotten and over with—

BUTTERWORTH: As a classics scholar, my training allowed me the ability to examine minutiae, detail, subtle relationships of some complexity. I have, or had, a particular ability to also expand my focus to the bigger picture. I come across a certain caesura in a line of Milton, say, or Spenser, and take note of it and then fit that observation—that detail—into the context of a literary—even linguistic—epoch—

ATTORNEY: It was, of course, a travesty of the worst kind. I am a civil libertarian, always have been. You could say I am an extremist for the Bill of Rights. My passion is protecting the First Amendment, which, by the way, is always under threat—

CANWELL: I'm always surprised how long it takes to catch up with the truth sometimes. How does a one-term legislator, and very unpopular because of what I determined to do, and did, I think rather well—there were many people who didn't agree with me. They weren't all Communist. Now, I'll name some for you if you wish that I do so—

BUTTERWORTH: Then I read Marx. Cataclysmic. He looks down at the human condition from such height—from above the stratosphere. He sees the human condition with such ease, such miraculous perspective, and without illusion. His originality. Not since . . . not since Shakespeare—in a totally different realm—has someone come along with such unfettered—with such unlimited vision and breadth of comprehension—

ATTORNEY: —What they did to these people. The legislature, the university, the press, the power structure in Seattle. Appalling. But even I have to admit, the times were . . . they were frightening. Scary. You carried a feeling around in your gut—

CANWELL: —I realized they were a bunch of weaklings.

BUTTERWORTH: Marx's analytic abilities defy comparison. And this above all—his conclusions demand, not simply debate, but action. Action from a wholly unheard of population. The underclass.

ATTORNEY: I remember being frightened of what both sides might do—what they might be capable of—pushing the goddamned button. I mean no matter what people say now, we were all in a dark tunnel and nobody knew what lay at the other end. That was the early Cold War.

CANWELL: What is education? It's an accumulation of facts, dissemination of information. I would like to have hit the Commies harder than I did. I would have liked to give the Communists a harder whack. We just barely scratched the surface. Professors were taking orders directly from superiors in the Communist Party—they were sheep killing dogs—

BUTTERWORTH: Once someone comes up with the observation that "the history of all hitherto existing society is the history of class struggle," you have unleashed not just thought but an onslaught, you have masses of people rushing in, to urge the inevitable—revolution. Why? So that justice can triumph—for *all*—

ATTORNEY: And there was something simultaneously blithe and fearful going on within many Americans. Common sense evaporated. The mainstream—that great and reliable mass of ordinary Americans, who had just won the war—was averting its gaze—or should I say shifting its gaze—to other things:

the almost desperate acquisition of the trappings of prosperity.

CANWELL: Communism is not a philosophy. It's an international conspiracy, a criminal conspiracy—a brilliant piece of work—

BUTTERWORTH: —Communism. We became the future. Our minds and spirits exploded with a new and irrefutable science of human intercourse. Goddammit, my comrades were wonderful. The Party had among its members the brightest, the most generous, the hardest working, the most moral, and the most courageous human beings I ever encountered.

ATTORNEY: Communism. Even the ACLU cleaned house. We threw out our own Reds. We didn't want to lose our credibility. Being a Communist was a very dangerous thing to be after the war. A lot of good people were ruined.

CANWELL: There wasn't anyone who was falsely tried. No one was mistreated at those trials despite what you may have heard. They should have fired more of them.

BUTTERWORTH: Later, it all went to shit. It cost me my wife, my son, my job, my health, my reputation, my effectiveness in the world—but these are not the issues. Objectively, I recognize that there are bound to be many casualties in epoch-making conflicts. Regardless, the principles of Socialism remain. They always will. They will come to pass. Mark my words. If the planet survives, it will have to deal with human justice at its elemental core. The truth will out.

ATTORNEY: Truth is, America has a tough time looking at itself honestly.

CANWELL: All I want is a truthful account of what I did.

[BLACKOUT]

SUPERTITLE:

THEATRE OF RECORD

National Guard Armory, Seattle, Washington

1948

Lights up to reveal the setting, which is divided into several areas, but the largest, most prominent is the hearing room in the 146th Field Artillery Building. The hearing room spills out, merging with the audience. Other areas, in darkness at the beginning of the play, exist to the sides, behind, and, perhaps, above the hearing room. There are screens of various sizes for projecting titles, documents, and photos. The hearing room accommodates the committee, its investigators, assistants, a court reporter, uniformed members of the Washington State Patrol, subpoenaed witnesses, and their attorneys. Most prominent in the hearing room are two long, elevated tables, set end to end with several microphones, behind which will sit the CHAIRMAN *and his* COMMITTEE *of six. Near the audience or in a front corner of the house are* MEMBERS OF THE PRESS, *including two* PHOTOGRAPHERS.*

Downstage and to the side of the committee table is a small table with a microphone and chair for chief investigator HOUSTON. *Near him sits a* COURT REPORTER. *Opposite and slightly elevated are two wooden chairs but no table, for subpoenaed witnesses and their counsels.*

There is the impression of large windows on one wall. Periodically, sounds of demonstrations from the street below filter into the hearing room. A U.S. and a Washington State flag are displayed. The effect should be of makeshift and sterile utility rather than a typical courtroom.

Throughout the hearing, ASSISTANTS, ATTORNEYS, WITNESSES, *and* COMMITTEE MEMBERS *come and go, attending to various tasks relating to the proceedings. Therefore, some movement and activity not directly related to the moment at hand take place.* WITNESSES *(and audience members who have been asked to "stand" as witnesses) are seated randomly within the audience.*

The hearing is about to commence, and present in the hearing room are HOUSTON, *the* COURT REPORTER, *and two Washington State* PATROLMEN, *who face the audience at "parade rest"—as they will throughout the hearing.*

PHOTOGRAPHERS *selectively take flash photos of* WITNESSES *seated with the audience. An* ASSISTANT *brings a folder to* HOUSTON *and exits.*

As house lights dim, SENATOR BIENZ *enters formally, stops center stage, and reads.*

SENATOR BIENZ: Whereas, these are times of public danger, subversive persons and groups are endangering our domestic unity, so as to leave us unprepared to meet aggression, and under cover of the protection afforded by the Bill of Rights these persons and groups seek to destroy our liberties and our freedom and to subject us to the domination of foreign powers. Now therefore be it resolved, that there is hereby created a Joint Legislative Fact-finding Committee on Un-American Activities in the State of Washington which shall investigate, ascertain, collate, and appraise all facts concerning individuals, groups or organizations whose activities are such as to undermine the stability of our American institutions: confuse and mislead the people. And be it further resolved that the Committee hereby created shall have all powers necessary or convenient to accomplish the objects and purposes of this resolution.

(BIENZ *steps aside and the rest of the* COMMITTEE MEMBERS *enter formally, in military fashion, escorted by a third* PATROLMAN. *They sit at the long tables. The* PATROLMAN *stands aside. Chairman* CANWELL, *seated, looks around and gavels loudly. Pause.*)

CANWELL: The committee will come to order. The public hearing of the Washington State Legislative Committee on Un-American Activities is now in session. Before we proceed, I wish to state that we will proceed with proper dignity here; no demonstrations will be tolerated. We are not going to debate the constitutionality of this committee or its method of procedure. Will you proceed, Mr. Houston?

(HOUSTON *rises, acknowledges Chairman* CANWELL, *picks up a list, and faces front.*)

HOUSTON: Will the following witnesses who have been subpoenaed rise when your name is called. Ted Astley. (ASTLEY *stands, as do the other witnesses, including audience member surrogates, when their names are called.*) Maud Beal. Joseph Butterworth. Joseph Cohen. Edwin Harold Eby. Mrs. Lena Eby. Clarissa Ethel. Garland Ethel. Ralph H. Gundlach. Mrs. Elizabeth D. Jacobs. Melville Jacobs. Burton James. Mrs. Florence Bean James. Albert M. Ottenheimer. Dr. Angelo Pellegrini. Herbert J. Phillips.

(*Attorney* JOHN CAUGHLAN *rises.*)

CAUGHLAN (*holding out letter*): I wish to advise you, sir, that Mr. Phillips is teaching at Columbia . . .

(CANWELL *gavels several times.*)

CANWELL: We are well aware of Mr. Phillips' position. Proceed,

Mr. Houston.

HOUSTON (*continuing from list*): Melvin M. Rader. Dr. Sophus Keith Winther. Mrs. Sophus Keith Winther.

(*A* STUDENT DEMONSTRATOR *stands and shouts from audience.*)

DEMONSTRATOR: Mr. Canwell, members of the committee, I'd like to read a statement—(CANWELL *gavels; the* DEMONSTRATOR *tries to shout over.*)—a statement that will expose these hearings for what they are!

CANWELL: Mister State Patrolman, if we do not have order, clear the room!

DEMONSTRATOR: This hearing is a farce! It's unconstit—

CANWELL (*gaveling*): —Anyone making a demonstration will be removed. Now those in this room—

DEMONSTRATOR: —constitutional and a witch-hunt. As an American citizen, I protest—

CANWELL (*to everyone*): If you wish to stay here, appear here as American citizens. (*A* PATROLMAN *reaches the* DEMONSTRATOR *and begins to restrain him or her.*) In the matter brought before this hearing you may stay. Otherwise you will be removed.

(*The* PATROLMAN *is joined by a* SECOND PATROLMAN; *they drag the* DEMONSTRATOR *through the crowd and out of the auditorium.*)

DEMONSTRATOR: —You have no right. Let me go! You see? This is your committee—

CANWELL: There will be no compromise on that. (*He gavels again.*) This meeting will proceed in an orderly manner, if you are all taken out!

(*Light bulbs flash as* REPORTERS *run to the altercation. The young* DEMONSTRATOR *is removed from hearing as gavel pounds.*)

[BLACKOUT]

SUPERTITLE:

THEATRE OF CONJECTURE

The City Desk

Two months before the hearings

On one of the projection screens appears the 1948 masthead of the Seattle Post-Intelligencer. *Another screen shows the headline and part of the story "Bienz Claims 150 Reds on Campus."*

The city desk room of the Seattle P-I. *Desks, clutter, noir lighting. As lights come up we see newspaper columnist* CONRAD CURLEW *typing and, at another desk, editorial assistant* VIOLA JAEGER *reading from a file and making notes. After a moment* FRED NIENDORFF, *business editor, enters escorting* CANWELL.

NIENDORFF: Everyone else has gone home. We won't be disturbed here.

CANWELL: Hmm. What about those two?

NIENDORFF: They're working with me. I'll introduce—

CANWELL: —I don't like this.

NIENDORFF: General Ashley requested we meet here, Al.

CANWELL: Well where is he?

NIENDORFF: At the Legion banquet. He'll be here.

CANWELL: When?

NIENDORFF: I don't know. Now. Soon. He's going back to D.C. tonight.

CANWELL: They fly East at night?

NIENDORFF: He's a general, Al. He flies anytime he wants to. What are you—

CANWELL: —These *people*. You drag me down here—I can't conduct committee business in a newspaper office—

NIENDORFF: —This is a casual meeting. Unofficial. General Ashley calls me at home, says he wants to meet the head honcho of the committee, says he'll drop by the newspaper office—that's the whole conversation. I figure if he wants to meet you, he's got his reasons. I said I'd get you here. You're here. He's coming. What's the matter?

CANWELL: I don't know who these . . . this young woman. Him. I think—I think I should go and you bring the general to my office. It's only a few blocks. We can talk frankly there.

NIENDORFF: Here. Let me introduce you. This is Vi.

VIOLA: Hello, Senator, honored to meetcha—

NIENDORFF: Uh . . . Chairman Canwell is a member of the *House*. (*Calling across the room*) Conrad, when's the lock?

VIOLA: Oh. Sorry—

CANWELL: —not important, Miss . . .

CURLEW: Twenty-eight minutes.

VIOLA: Everyone calls me "Vi"—

NIENDORFF (*to* CANWELL): —We gotta hurry. Got something to show you, Al, we want to bring—

CANWELL (*to* NIENDORFF): —So you've drawn up a list?

NIENDORFF: Yes. Viola did.

CANWELL: This woman is determining who my committee is going to subpoena?

CURLEW: She's the only one with the patience to sort through all the information—

VIOLA: It wasn't that difficult. I just made a graph.

CANWELL: Graph?

NIENDORFF: She figured out—

VIOLA: —I just cross-matched people's names with how many communist fronts and petitions they were associated with. It was simple really.

CANWELL: How many names made it on your list?

NIENDORFF: A lot fewer than Bienz's number. We've prepared a story—

CANWELL: —Senator Bienz is not reliable. He's an extremist—

VIOLA: —I came up with thirty names.

CANWELL: Thirty.

VIOLA: Yes, I figured—

NIENDORFF: —We decided a minimum of three fronts or five petitions was a good cutting-off—

CANWELL: —Let me see it.

VIOLA: The list?

CANWELL: Yes.

VIOLA (*handing it to him*): It's not typed yet—

CANWELL: That's all right. (*Looks at it*) You've a good hand. (*As he reads*) What's your last name, Miss . . . ?

VIOLA: Uh, it's . . . Mrs., actually. Jaeger. But "Vi" works just as well.

CANWELL: Let's see . . . Butterworth, Eby, Ethel, Gundlach . . . good . . .

NIENDORFF: I thought you'd approve—

CANWELL: —you've even got 'em alphabetized—the Jameses, Phillips, Rader. Excellent. I prefer calling you by your last name. Don't like to see women in this line of . . .

VIOLA: Well, I look life straight in the eye.

CURLEW (*approaching*): She's nobody's fool, Mr. Canwell. I'm Conrad Curlew. Welcome to Dodge City.

CANWELL: What?

CURLEW: My little joke. You've come across the mountains to clean up our little town.

CANWELL: Curlew. You write a column, don't you?

CURLEW: Oh yes. Yes. I'm Mr. Hearst's local mouthpiece. My soul belongs to Daddy.

NIENDORFF: Pay no attention to him, Al. Conrad fancies himself a cynic, but he's just—

CANWELL: —Mr. Hearst has been very good to me. (*To* VIOLA) This is a nice piece of work.

VIOLA: I'm flattered you like it.

NIENDORFF: Well, Conrad and I have a story ready to go to press right now with this new number. We want to attribute the number to you—

CANWELL: —You're not printing any of these names are you?

NIENDORFF: Oh, no, no, no. Only yours. Give him the story, Conrad. We've been working all day—

CANWELL: —Don't go publishing any names. This is an above-board operation. I smell alcohol. Someone been drinking?

NIENDORFF (*shooting a glance toward* CURLEW): This is what we're about to send to linotype. Viola, why don't you type up our list in triplicate. (CANWELL *looks at article.* VIOLA *starts for her desk.*) You see, between now and the hearings we plan to make discreet disclosures—on a daily basis.

CANWELL: Do you have children, Mrs . . . uh . . . Jaeger?

VIOLA: No. I was married only a very short time.

CANWELL: Do you attend church?

VIOLA: Church? Oh, sure. Used to. More or less stopped when I was married—but that was only for four months. Not that much lately. Been awfully busy—

CANWELL: —You said you look life straight in the eye, and that's good. You should try looking *God* straight in the eye sometime. It's blinding. (*He goes back to reading.*)

VIOLA: Oh. (*Beat*) Excuse . . . me . . . (*She continues toward her desk to finish typing the list.*)

CURLEW (*taking a bottle from his desk*): Congratulations, Vi, my dear, you seem to have pleased the chairman. I'd like to offer a toast—

NIENDORFF: Put the bottle away, Conrad—

CURLEW: —to offer a toast to the lady of the hour.

NIENDORFF: We still have work to do—

CURLEW: —I consider this unpaid overtime—

NIENDORFF: —Don't you dare get drunk. We need you. The general—

CURLEW: —I have about thirty minutes of sobriety left. No more. The clock is ticking. (*Holding up the bottle*) Anyone want a slug?

CANWELL: You let your employees drink on the job?

NIENDORFF: I am not his boss—or his keeper.

CANWELL: You people live a different life over here in Seattle.

CURLEW: Really? Well, if the bottle goes, I go with it. (*He moves back toward his desk.*)

NIENDORFF (*changing subject*): You notice the way we say, "among those subpoenaed will be figures from a local theatre company," without mentioning their names?

CANWELL: Hmmm.

NIENDORFF: We appear discreet. That's our strategy. Always imply we know more than we write about. That way we protect the good names of the people we . . . (*He chuckles.*) well, the people we eventually expose.

CURLEW: You want a drink, Vi?

VIOLA: Oh, sure. Just a teeny one. (*Noticing* CANWELL's *glance at her*) I have a cup from the watercooler right here in my purse somewhere. See? (*They are all looking at her.*) Sometimes I get headaches.

CANWELL: I don't think you should do that. This is official business—and . . . ah . . . you are in some way . . . an agent of the

State by being here. In this company. Whether you know it or
not. You all are.

VIOLA: I am?

NIENDORFF: We are?

CANWELL: Yes. In a sense . . . you all are. This is an immensely
sensitive activity we are engaged in here—and yes, I would
invoke that you are all acting in a semideputized capacity. In a
sense. Yes.

VIOLA: Oh. I didn't get that I was. I thought . . . we . . . we were
informally . . . I thought we were under newspaper rules, not
some other kind of—I thought I was here sort of as a favor to
Mr. Niendorff? Otherwise I would either be at home, or our
time here together would involve . . . you know . . . *recompense*
of some kind. I'm sorry Mr. Canwell, Your Honor, but I have
been up since 5 A.M. and was asked to stay late because Mr.
Bienz's comments over in Spokane, and this was considered an
emergency by my boss here, Mr. Niendorff. And I have worked
all day for my forty-five dollars a week and this is *my* time—

NIENDORFF: —There, there, Vi, calm down. She's tired—

CANWELL: —fine, young lady. You are free to do as you wish. "It's
your misfortune and none of my own." Let's get on with this.
Fred, don't ever ask me to come here—

(*U.S. Air Force General* WALTER J. ASHLEY *enters with two* MILI-
TARY ESCORTS.)

ASHLEY: D'you jackasses know that the goddamned door to this
building gets locked at nine o'clock?

NIENDORFF: Oh my god, General, I forgot—

ASHLEY: —We had to scout up your goddamned janitor for God's
sake. We've been outside with our thumbs up our asses, waiting for some goddamned Mexican to open up the joint—

NIENDORFF: —I'm terribly sorry, I completely—

ASHLEY: —This is not the way to remain on good terms with the Pentagon.

NIENDORFF: Tell me what I can do to—

ASHLEY: —What gives here?

NIENDORFF: General. First, please accept my apologies, I have no excuses. Next let me say, this is an honor, not only for myself, but on behalf of the whole *Post-Intelligencer*—

ASHLEY: —Yes. However, since nobody is going to know I dropped in here tonight . . . the degree to which honor is a factor here will be limited to . . . we present few. Comprende? You the Chairman? Cantwell?

CANWELL: *Can*-well. Yes. Pleased to—

ASHLEY: —As long as I was in town, I thought I'd drop by to express my support, et cetera, for your efforts.

CANWELL: Well, I'm most appreciative. I was invited to the banquet myself, but work prevented me—I hope—

ASHLEY: —Who're these folks?

NIENDORFF: My team. Mr. Curlew. Viola—

ASHLEY: —No loose lips here?

NIENDORFF: —We are all—

ASHLEY: —Fine, fine. You boys wait outside. (*His* ESCORTS *leave.*) Everything said here tonight is in confidence, unofficial, off the record. Understood?

CANWELL: —Actually, General, I'd much prefer that you and I go on over to my office. It's just up in the armory building—we could talk with complete security. I would enjoy—

ASHLEY: —I'm afraid not. Short on time. Flying back tonight. Now, what the hell you boys gonna do come . . . June, is it? You gonna spill some blood? Make the Commies in this state hurt— or you just gonna ruffle a few feathers?

CANWELL (*bristling*): Well, General, I think you can count on us—

ASHLEY: —I hope you boys aren't in over your heads. That's what I hope. You back off . . . you show mercy . . . they'll cut your throats. Now—what we have here is an opportunity to set an example—for the rest of the country. These state-run committees can be very useful. Grass roots, et cetera. If you guys are seen dragging these suckers out into the street and shoving flashlights down their throats—the public will pay attention. So far they're not. They are buying automobiles, homes, television sets. No thought for yesterday. No thought for tomorrow. The war is becoming a vague memory. Among the few who do pay attention, *our* fair state . . . is a laughingstock.

CANWELL: Well, I aim to fix that, General. That's why I ran for office.

ASHLEY: You did? Know what I bet? I'll bet you ran for office like all of them. You got a boner for it.

CANWELL: General! (*They all look at* CANWELL.) There is a lady present.

ASHLEY: What? (*Giving* VIOLA *a once-over*) Oh yes, of course . . . what . . . ever. I figure she's here, she's tough. No?

VIOLA: I wasn't born yesterday.

ASHLEY: Where were we?

CANWELL: With all due respect sir, I think our perspectives are a little different—yours and mine. I would be less than honest if I didn't point out that I take fierce pride in the fact that no one and no organization—not even the American Legion— can match the depth and range of my personal investigations of communism in the Pacific Northwest. I guarantee I will deliver up to you domestic Communists and Party-liners of every stripe and shade. They will be known to you. It is up to you fellows on the national scene to take it from there. If domestic blood is going to be spilled, the federal government is going to have to take the lead. That's up to you and your friends in Washington, D.C. Talk to your bosses, General, talk to the Joint Chiefs, talk to Mr. Truman. That's what I have to say.

NIENDORFF: Al, I think the general is doing his job—

CANWELL: —Excuse me, but I am a frank man.

ASHLEY: A relative virtue in my experience. Convincing talk is better than frank talk. I've been doing a fair amount of the latter aimed at a certain, highly placed, elected official. And I would conclude from all this . . . talk . . . that this high official needs to be convinced that the domestic communist threat from within our borders is . . . *real.* That it is *pervasive.* That it is *dangerous.* The way I see it, *my* job is to convince him that *foreign* communism is an external threat to the U.S., even greater than fascism was. *Your* job is to convince the public that there is a concurrent *internal* threat. A massive threat from those among us—American citizens—from within our borders. You reading me?

CANWELL: I think we understand each other.

NIENDORFF: I want you to know, General, that we here at the *P-I* are also aware of the great potential for an even greater partnership between the new Air Force, the Boeing Company, and the city of Seattle. We are in the dawn of a new age—

ASHLEY: —You're not gonna see much of a fuckin' dawn as long as this area is regarded as a radical backwater. Back in D.C. they don't like this place—"the forty-seven states and the soviet of Washington," for Chrissake.

NIENDORFF: We accept it as our mandate to change that perception.

CANWELL: And I want you to know that I have evidence, I have files, I have information—

ASHLEY: —You told me—

CANWELL: —All through the thirties and since. The automobile strikes in Detroit—I was *there.* Harry Bridges' waterfront, here in Seattle—I *covered* it. Marx in the libraries—I know who *reads* him.

ASHLEY: I know I have a dick between my legs. It's what I do with it that counts. Sorry, Miss. Is that whiskey?

CURLEW: Well, gee, yes it is, I must confess . . . uh . . . if you don't court-martial me, I'll offer you a drink.

ASHLEY: I'll take a snort. (*Offering the bottle*) Young lady?

VIOLA (*retrieving her paper cup from her purse*): Thank you. Just a drop.

ASHLEY: To the committee. Thank you. What's your—

CURLEW: —It's Curlew, General. Like the bird. Help yourself. Vi, you'd better get this over to linotype before the lock.

VIOLA: Uh . . . sure. I'll be right back.

ASHLEY: Why doesn't the little lady take a hike. What say?

VIOLA: Oh. You want me to leave?

ASHLEY: Something like that.

NIENDORFF: You can go home, Vi.

VIOLA: Oh. I see.

CURLEW: I'm going over to the Grove for a nightcap when we finish here.

VIOLA: Mmm. Well. Goodnight.

(VIOLA *exits.*)

CANWELL: Well, General, if you're as busy as I am—

ASHLEY (*interrupting*): —I can get you a national witness.

CANWELL: What?

ASHLEY: A significant . . . presence for your little show.

NIENDORFF: What sort of witness?

ASHLEY: A big one. Friendly.

CANWELL: We have a lot of friendly witnesses already—

ASHLEY: —Not this one, you don't. A Negro and a Soviet. An

American-born nigger who lived in goddamned Moscow for several years before the war—an expatriate. One of Stalin's ornaments. There's pictures of 'em together. The poor sap got disillusioned. Came back to the States, started attacking certain policies of the American Communist Party, so they demoted him. He quit the Party. FBI tried, couldn't get to him. They waited. Finally he got married, hadda coupla kids. There was some kinda incident. Anyway, he's ours. He is friendly, he's credible, he's even *flexible*—if you know what I mean. We don't want to spread him too thin. I can get him for you. It's your call.

CANWELL: General, that's a very generous offer on your part and I appreciate it. I just don't think we need him. He'd just take time away from the white witnesses—

ASHLEY: It's your call. (*To* NIENDORFF) Is he for real? This guy's a gold mine. He's been everywhere, including a secret Commie school in upstate New York. It's not a secret anymore. He can place just about anyone you want, any*where* you want, when*ever* you want 'em to have been there.

CANWELL: I don't have the greatest confidence in most Negroes—

CURLEW: Excuse me, Mr. Canwell, I think you're overlooking— we are talking about the possibility of conspiracy here.

CANWELL: This is a conspiracy?

CURLEW: No, not us—well, maybe us, maybe us too. But that's a different conversation. (*He laughs.*) I love this. Probably us too. Yes. No. But listen. It seems to me this is an opportunity to use the hearings to expose a larger conspiracy, a web of intrigue— a spy story. See, the trouble is, the way you have the hearings geared now, you essentially only have ideological differences. Name calling. Smearing.

CANWELL: I knew you'd talk nonsense sooner or later. These hearings are going to be magnifi—

ASHLEY: —He's right. No matter how much you smear people, you haven't got a *crime*.

CANWELL: Of course we do! We have the crime of contempt for anyone who refuses—

ASHLEY: —Regardless of what you wish, no one is going to believe a bunch of egghead professors are capable of doing any real harm—unless you can expose them as liars, as engaging in secret activities outside this region. Otherwise, it won't wash. But—and this is where this George Hewitt comes in—if you can get actual testimony against a couple of them, accusing them of leading double lives, engaging in conspiracy, not just in their basements and attics, but around the country—internationally—

CURLEW: —Phillips, Gundlach, the Jameses. Even Rader—

CANWELL: —Rader?

CURLEW: —A nice, respectable liberal, looks like the family doctor, smells of integrity—

CANWELL: —He grew up in my neck of the woods—farm kid who's father despaired of making him a farmer. Went to college instead. I investigated him on my own, years ago.

CURLEW: And you blindside him with evidence of a whole other, secret life—

CANWELL: —Too easy. I don't think—

CURLEW: —No cross-examination of the accuser, no rebuttal. You got headlines, you have the whole institution of the university rocked—a whipsaw. Everyone afraid of his neighbors. Suspicion everywhere.

CANWELL: I don't think so.

NIENDORFF: Why not, Al?

CANWELL: Using the Negro's testimony would be too risky. I have my own information on Rader. I wouldn't trust an outsider. Especially—

ASHLEY: —His credibility is one hundred percent. Immigration is throwing the foreign born out of the country right and left based on his testimony. I'll tell you what, fella, you are looking a gift horse in the mouth.

NIENDORFF: Think about it, Al. When it's all over, you win the door prize. A ticket to higher political office.

CANWELL: That's not why I'm doing this. Is that clear? I am a patriot. I happen to believe there is a God looking down on all this. (*Pause*) I don't think so. It's too risky.

ASHLEY: Too risky. My job in the last war was to win. We won. Let me tell you something about patriotism, Mr. Chairman. Let me tell you about risk. Let me tell you about . . . *winning*. I cut my teeth on sending boys in B-17s over Germany. *Before* fighter escort planes accompanied them. My job was to calculate how many young men, how many planes it would take to create a *surplus*—a surplus of young American airmen so that not *all* would be shot down. Not all would fall out of the fucking sky. Only most. And therefore *some* bombs would make it to their targets. The *surplus* as we called it—it was the little joke among us commanders—became metal, fire, and flesh. Junk falling from the sky. Over twenty thousand of those men *disintegrated*. I . . . I want you to know that I *personally* . . . helped design and carry out that strategy. I did it consciously—and I did it deliberately. Let me tell you about God. I *was* God. Every day, lives and burning planes falling out of the sky because of me. Everything just one stop ahead of chaos. That's how I cut my teeth. Then I was assigned to the Pacific, where I helped figure out how to use airpower to beat the Japs. Simple. Cheat. We made sure that raids on Japan inflicted maximum *civilian* casualties. More firebombing. Military targets became incidental and cover for the real policy: cremate the *populace*. You know why? So that after the war Stalin would have no doubt that we are vicious enough and have the balls to carry out any policy we choose in order to dominate the fucking world. Now I've been asked to serve in the highest echelons. You know why? Because I *understand* the enemy. And I play for keeps. But we have inherited a complacent population. So, you see, it's up to you. If you manage to create panic in the streets about this, Washington will have to pay attention. Then you can count me as your friend. If not, you can wipe my ass with your patriotism, your God, and your . . . professors. Talk about surplus. Fred, if you decide you want Hewitt, wire me at the Pentagon with this message: "We'd like the minstrel show in Seattle, on such and such a date." We'll ship him here, airfreight. Good night. (*Going to door, he opens it.*) C'mon, boys, see if you can figure out how to get me outta this fuckin' building.

(ASHLEY *exits, silence.*)

CURLEW: Not exactly the Mahatma Gandhi.

NIENDORFF (*silence*): Whaddya say, Al?

CANWELL: He's a scarred man and full of—(*Pause*). Of course, he's right about this. We are either strong enough for this work or we don't deserve—there's no middle ground. I have children, I have a farm and a wife. Hmm. Rader. I didn't come up with much when I . . . I know he was approached by a Party recruiter, but . . . maybe I overlooked something. Maybe Rader is part of it all.

CURLEW: Especially if we decide he is.

NIENDORFF: Shut up, Conrad. You're drunk. From this moment forward we should proceed with the assumption that Rader is a secret member of the Party. Period.

CANWELL: It makes perfect sense. He stays out of the sewer but is part of the sewer.

CURLEW: And he isn't the only one. (NIENDORFF *shoots him a glance.* CURLEW *lifts his glass.*)

CANWELL (*ignoring* CURLEW): The idea of the colored fellow still makes me nervous. What's his name?

NIENDORFF: Hewitt, I believe.

CANWELL: I don't trust—I am getting sure about Rader, though.

CURLEW: Here's to you Melvin Rader. Welcome to the big time. (*To the others*) I am much more comfortable now that we have—what would you call it?—*help* from on high. It's clear. I think it's safe to say that we are moving away from any hope of kidding ourselves to actual, clear, fully conscious, undeniable—

NIENDORFF: Will you just shut up! Go home! Your day is done.

CANWELL: I don't like a drunk. Not even a little. (*Pause*) Y'know, Fred, there's no doubt but that we have our work cut out for us. This is the beginning of something bigger than any of us. I believe we are entering into a . . . into combat against citizen traitors. Not since the Civil War . . . (*Musing*) Don't let anyone kid you. (*Pause*) If we are gonna win, we have to do as the general says: go for broke. God bless America.

[BLACKOUT]

A middle-aged man in a Borsalino hat and an old trench coat, JOSEPH BUTTERWORTH, *enters stage right, leading his somewhat mentally retarded son,* JOEY. *They move slowly, Butoh-like, toward stage left. Their journey across the stage is not complete until the following speeches are completed. There is a low percussive sound throughout this progression.*

SUPERTITLE:
THEATRE OF RECORD
Senator Thomas Bienz

Senator BIENZ *stands in a pool of light, addressing someone beyond audience.*

BIENZ: My statement was not meant to smear the university. It was meant to call attention to conditions and help the Regents clean house.

[LIGHTS OUT]

SUPERTITLE:
THEATRE OF RECORD
Seattle Post-Intelligencer
April 6, 1948

NIENDORFF (*sitting at a typewriter*): By mutual arrangement, Mr. Canwell met with the Board of Regents. The Board expressed itself unanimously that it welcomes this investigation. The Board assured Mr. Canwell that if evidence is presented showing beyond any doubt any faculty member to be engaged in subversive activity, it would move immediately for such member's dismissal.

[LIGHTS OUT]

SUPERTITLE:

THEATRE OF RECORD

Raymond B. Allen, President, University of Washington

1948

ALLEN (*in a pool of light looking out beyond audience*): The university's problem is a complex one. Members of the Communist Party are not free men but rather accept the dictation of an extreme political dogma and perhaps even that of a foreign power. The university has attempted not to prejudge these issues, but it cannot ignore them. Taking cognizance of these issues does not abridge academic freedom. Charges made in some quarters that the committee has engaged in a "witch-hunt" must be examined in the light of the fact that the committee has not sought to elicit testimony on the political or social views of faculty members other than from those who, for some concrete reason, were believed to be or to have been members of the Communist Party.

[LIGHTS OUT]

Rhythmic, percussive sound continues as the two figures, JOE *and* JOEY BUTTERWORTH, *reach the other side of the stage.* BUTTERWORTH *seems to be opening a door. A shaft of light illuminates a middle-aged woman hanged from a makeshift noose. An overturned kitchen chair, her hat and purse, lie beneath her body.* BUTTERWORTH *is still. The boy,* JOEY, *looking at his mother, tries to circle his father, tugging at him gently like a tethered boat.* JOEY *makes a low, subdued sound.* BUTTERWORTH *simply looks at the corpse. Pause.*

[BLACKOUT]

SUPERTITLE:
THEATRE OF RECORD
Albert Canwell
1995

CANWELL (*in a pool of light*): Well, most cases, I selected the two ablest men I had. They were advised to be discreet and courteous to these people and in general. They'd say, "The chairman would like you to come down to the office, talk to him." And in every case, they were courteously approached and invited to come down and state their position and I had agreed with Dr. Allen, the president, that I would tell him in advance who I was going to subpoena and so I did and so there weren't any surprises pulled on these people. Nobody was roughed up like they used to—circulated stories that that happened, but it didn't. They were treated so much better than they were entitled to by their conduct.

[BLACKOUT]

SUPERTITLE:
THEATRE OF CONJECTURE
The Visit
April 1948

Professor JOSEPH BUTTERWORTH'S *office at the University of Washington. His desk and surroundings show years of focus on things other than neatness. Amid the clutter is a nearly full ashtray and a water glass. Upstage is a door with a frosted-glass panel. A transom above.* BUTTERWORTH *sits at his desk. His friend and colleague* MAUD BEAL *is standing. They are somewhat formal and reticent with one another.*

BEAL: I just don't get it Joe. Why would she kill herself?

BUTTERWORTH: I don't know.

BEAL: I thought—you think you know someone . . .

BUTTERWORTH: I know.

BEAL: And then you realize . . . (*Pause*)

BUTTERWORTH: What?

BEAL: You realize . . . you realize you've been blind to what's right in front of you. The clues must have—

BUTTERWORTH: —Hmm, yes . . .

BEAL: Is that true of you?

BUTTERWORTH: Yes, I suppose so. I wasn't prepared for this . . . (*Pause*) No. But we have to move on, Maud.

BEAL: She left no clues as to why?

BUTTERWORTH: It is utterly enigmatic. Of course, one does look back with altered eyes . . . but we have to move on, you know. The boy.

BEAL: Joey.

BUTTERWORTH: The boy needs to move on. He can't comprehend the actuality . . . or perhaps he can—and does—and *I'm* the one . . . (*Shrugging, silence*)

BEAL: I'd like to help. I don't know children. Joey doesn't seem like—

BUTTERWORTH: —No. Joey is not like—Joey is his own—uh . . . somewhat unique.

BEAL: He must be devastated underneath it all.

BUTTERWORTH: It's like some grotesque Halloween prank to him. He's ghoulish. "Did her eyes pop out?" he asks. "Is she rotting yet?" Concrete questions.

BEAL: Joe, what are you going to do with . . . ?

BUTTERWORTH: Going to do with him?

BEAL: Yes.

(*There is a knock at the door.*)

BUTTERWORTH: My office hours. A student.

BEAL: Yes. (*Starting for door*) Is there anything I can . . . ?

BUTTERWORTH: Joey likes it that you grow devil's foot in your garden. Perhaps he and I could take a bus out to Bothell for a visit?

BEAL: Please come anytime.

(BEAL *opens the door and* HOUSTON *appears. He wears a western style suit and boots. She takes him in, glances back at* BUTTERWORTH *as she exits.*)

HOUSTON: Joseph Butterworth?

BUTTERWORTH: Yes?

HOUSTON (*opening door wider, revealing a second man,* MORROW JEWELL): Do you have a moment?

BUTTERWORTH: Do I know you—? (*Squinting, taking off glasses, cleaning them*)

HOUSTON: —I don't think so, not yet—

BUTTERWORTH: —a former student?

HOUSTON: No.

BUTTERWORTH: Oh no, perhaps not—

HOUSTON: —No. There are some issues we'd like to discuss—

BUTTERWORTH: —Who are you? I don't recall an appointment—

(*He takes out a cigarette.*)

HOUSTON: —Can we come in and shut the door? We'd like to—

BUTTERWORTH: —I don't understand.

HOUSTON (*snapping open a lidded lighter, he ignites and offers the flame, all in one movement*): We'd like to protect your privacy. Could we come in? Sit down?

BUTTERWORTH (*refusing the light, takes the cigarette out of his mouth, returns it to pack*): What do you want?

JEWELL: I'll just step in here and close the door. Okay, Mr. Butterworth? (*He does so.*)

BUTTERWORTH: Who are you fellows?

HOUSTON: We are with the state of Washington.

(*There is a pause while they look at each other.*)

BUTTERWORTH: I thought as much. Any particular branch?

HOUSTON: The legislature. (*A moment of silence*) I am Chief Investigator Houston. This is Mr. Jewell, private investigator and consultant to the committee.

JEWELL: How do you do?

BUTTERWORTH: Committee?

HOUSTON: On un-American—

BUTTERWORTH: —I understand—

HOUSTON: —activities.

JEWELL: Do you call yourself Doctor Butterworth or Professor Butterworth?

BUTTERWORTH: I'm Joe, to my friends.

JEWELL: Joe.

BUTTERWORTH: You can call me Professor.

JEWELL (*slight pause*): Professor. Okey-dokey.

BUTTERWORTH: To what do I owe this visit?

HOUSTON: Professor—

BUTTERWORTH: —You are intruding on my office hours. Students may be coming by—

HOUSTON: —We don't need much time with you right now. We

merely want to establish some areas for future discussion. Invite you to come see us. Can I sit down?

BUTTERWORTH: I really see no need to pursue this—

HOUSTON (*smiling*): —I think it's important that we chat a bit. Open some channels—

JEWELL: —Just a conversation—

BUTTERWORTH: —You don't understand. I'm not interested.

HOUSTON: We were sorry to hear about your wife's passing. You have our condolences.

JEWELL: Mine too.

BUTTERWORTH: Let me get this clear. You are *consoling* me?

JEWELL: We are . . . sympathetic to your plight.

HOUSTON: Morrow . . . not now. We want to be perfectly frank with you, Professor Butterworth. We are officials of the legislature. We have a job to do. But we do want to take into account your unfortunate circumstances.

BUTTERWORTH: How would you know—

HOUSTON: —Please let me finish, sir. We want to be sensitive to your situation. Yes, we were sorry to hear of your wife's demise. Those kinds of things are very hard on—well, on everybody. We want our discussion here to be—

BUTTERWORTH: —Discussion? We aren't going to have any discussion.

HOUSTON: Oh, I think so. I do.

BUTTERWORTH: I'd like you to leave now, please.

HOUSTON: We want to disrupt your life as little as possible. We are interested in working with you to keep any public embarrassment to a minimum. We want you to be able to get back to as normal a life as possible—both you and your son, in these new circumstances.

BUTTERWORTH: You don't seem to be hearing. I am bringing this meeting to a close.

HOUSTON: Oh, I hear you just fine. I want you to hear me. To hear us. You are at a crossroads. You could come out of this relatively unscathed. But we need you to be honest and candid with us.

BUTTERWORTH: Candid? Candor? From the Latin *candere,* "to kindle," in compound *incendere,* "to set fire to," "incendiary." (*He whispers with mock conspiracy:*) *Am I a fire monger? An arsonist? Your job would be easier!* (*Normal volume*) Could I borrow your lighter after all? No? Well, I believe I have a match. (*Taking out a cigarette and lighting it, he begins speaking very rapidly, seemingly lost in abstraction.*) I wouldn't presume to burden your time recounting the minutiae of my uh—glimmering—existence. However, if you are not to be discouraged, I suggest, in the interest of economy of motion, that you *read* me first—my published work—before we attempt a coherent discussion. I have authored several papers and articles which are part of the critical literature. You could begin by reading *The Faerie Queene* and then my dissertation-cum-book; it's a standard part of the reference literature on Spenser—and *use* it as a lens with which to examine the poem again and which should enable you to begin to grasp some of Spenser's syntactic subtleties, disguised in the fabric of his poetry—and how the embedded, almost subtextual meanings—sometimes contradictory but always cogent—*ignited,* in later poets, an *explosion* of linguistic advancements—more fireworks! (*He chuckles at his joke.*) You could then move on to my subsequent articles on the evolution of language. After which you might *write* me with your responses and inquiries, and I, or one of my teaching assistants, would be happy to engage in any discussion that is apt to arise. I look forward to reading your responses and your evaluation of my thoughts—and indeed my life's work.

JEWELL: See what I've been trying to tell you. These guys—you can't give 'em a break—they'd piss on their mothers.

HOUSTON: Please, Morrow. Please, let me—Mr. Butterworth, Professor. (*Beat*) We understand your son's going to be needing funds from Aid to Dependent Children. Is that true?

BUTTERWORTH (*pause*): Are you fellows in cahoots with the Welfare Office?

HOUSTON: Oh no, not at all. We're just trying to take into account your son's situation. He's not—he's a sort of a—handicapped person, is he not?

BUTTERWORTH: You've been spying on me. When have you—

HOUSTON: —I don't think you are taking us seriously. You are under investigation by the state of Washington—essentially for treason. Is that clear? Now, I want you to know that we do have the agency's ear, vis-à-vis your son. I happen to know they are compassionate about your son's difficulties, especially in light of your situation—of the trouble you are in.

BUTTERWORTH: You are blackmailing me with the boy's need for help.

HOUSTON: I assure you we can have no negative impact on your appeal for welfare funds for your son. All we might be able to do, on a strictly informal basis, would be to influence a *positive* outcome. Now, if you would be willing to come to our office—

BUTTERWORTH (*seeming to slump*): Tell me . . . what do you want from me?

HOUSTON: Mr. Butterworth. We are not interested in your academics. We don't want to touch them, you see? We are only interested in your outside activities. And only since about 1935, which is the time we are pretty certain you became interested and involved in the Communist Party USA. Your academic credentials are not at issue.

JEWELL: It's your little stamp collection we're after.

HOUSTON: You know, Professor, as painful as it might be to contemplate, a lot of what you are considering your personal and private activities are already part of the public record. And that record is growing by the day. I think it's safe to say your privacy as you knew it in the past is just that. A thing of the past. We simply want to cooperate with you in any way we can about your connections to the Party so as to cause as little pain and as little peril to you, and especially to your poor son.

BUTTERWORTH: Don't you worry about my son. I'll look after him.

HOUSTON: But don't you see? You aren't. You can't. You've already applied for public assistance for him—

BUTTERWORTH: Get out.

HOUSTON: —from the United States government.

BUTTERWORTH: You . . . shit-asses.

HOUSTON (*after a beat*): We don't have to become uncivilized here, Professor—

BUTTERWORTH: —eaters of shit.

JEWELL: We got a rise out of you, in any case. I'll tell you fella. You don't cooperate, you're gonna become famous.

HOUSTON: I wish you would reconsider. It's better that we work together. "Divided we fall."

JEWELL: You wanna be mentioned on Walter Winchell? Or get yourself on the cover of *Life Magazine*, trying to hide your face with your hat?

HOUSTON: Please. Don't get caught in this gully wash, sir.

BUTTERWORTH: All your guns out and see? My hands aren't even shaking. (*Rising, going to door*) Now, I am going to call the police to have you removed from my office.

(*He opens the door and two* STATE PATROLMEN *standing at parade rest, their backs to the door, turn around.* BUTTERWORTH *turns to* HOUSTON.)

HOUSTON: We had them posted here to protect our privacy. Yours and ours.

JEWELL: Maybe you wanna make a citizen's arrest? You better go home and have a drink, fella.

BUTTERWORTH: Are you aware the two of you are a parody of the Police State? (*They don't respond.*) You aren't, are you?

HOUSTON: I'll level with you, Butterworth. Basically, you are small potatoes. Our friends in the other Washington have already put film stars and scriptwriters out of commission and swept them, as your . . . friend, Karl Marx, says, "into the dustbin of history." Tell me, Professor, what is going to happen to the likes of you, if you don't cooperate? Give it some thought. Good day, Professor.

(HOUSTON *and* MORROW *exit. The* PATROLMEN *follow.*)

[LIGHTS FADE]

SUPERTITLE:

THEATRE OF RECORD

Albert Canwell

1994 Interview

CANWELL: I felt that this president of the university, who obviously was willing to cooperate with us, was convinced this was the way it should be done, because I told him when I first contacted him. If I didn't do this job, somebody else will, and I said somebody else might not be as conscientious or careful as I am, and Allen, I think, became convinced that that was the case and I gave him a list of the professors that we were going to subpoena, the ones that we knew to be Communist.

[BLACKOUT]

THEATRE OF CONJECTURE

A Stroll around Green Lake

1948

ANGELO PELLEGRINI *and* MELVIN RADER *enter. They slowly make their way across upstage. As they speak they move down-right and out the aisle.*

RADER: Your call was—disconcerting. Like a spy movie with Claude Rains. Meeting in the park at night, pretending nonchalance.

PELLEGRINI: Yeah. Life imitates schlock. Friends are telling me they are certain they're being tailed, their phones are making funny noises. Just like in the movies. Just like my recent dreams.

RADER: What is this—

PELLEGRINI: —I've been subpoenaed.

RADER (*stopping*): Oh dear. (*Walking again*) Oh dear.

PELLEGRINI: That's all you have to say, then. "Oh dear." How about "Oh shit"?

RADER: Yes. (*Pause*) Oh dear. When did this—

PELLEGRINI: —This morning.

RADER: Difficult. I imagine—

PELLEGRINI: —They asked me a lot of questions.

RADER: I don't know—I don't know what to make of it . . .

(RADER *and* PELLEGRINI *exit.*)

SUPERTITLE:

THEATRE OF CONJECTURE

Between the Devil and the Deep Blue

The Bronx, New York

1948

A suggestion of a small apartment bedroom of GEORGE *and* ALETHIA
HEWITT. *Sound of a baby crying in the next room.* ALETHIA, *pregnant in bed.* GEORGE, *getting dressed to go downtown.*

HEWITT: We gotta look reality right in the face. No other options, sweetheart.

ALETHIA: They're gonna make you do this for the rest of your days, aren't they?

HEWITT: Only as long as they pay.

ALETHIA: You sound like you think you gotta job.

HEWITT: Right. That's the way I'm looking at it. Employment. Business. I am learning to play those Feds like a fiddle.

ALETHIA: I'll tell you what. They are going to pick away till there's just pieces of you left.

HEWITT: They're gonna get nothing outta me that matters! Is that clear? Go get Lucy outta bed, will you? (*She doesn't move.*) My choices have to be very few for the time being, that's all. I got it under control, you hear? I am like an entertainer. I sing like bird. (*He tries to laugh.*) I can handle it.

ALETHIA (*getting out of bed*): Those men will chew you up and spit you out, if you don't jump when they tell you. Who're you tryin' to kid? Yourself? 'Cause you sure are not foolin' me. (*Calling into the next room as she puts on a robe*) I'll be there in a jif, sweetheart.

(*Lights out and up on* RADER *and* PELLEGRINI *reentering from another part of the stage.*)

PELLEGRINI: . . . you see, the implications are terrifying—and not only on a personal level. I mean the whole country.

RADER: Yes. These loyalty issues could lead to . . . I don't know . . . an unraveling of the whole social contract.

PELLEGRINI: It's hard to know where to land on this.

RADER: You mean whether or not to cooperate?

PELLEGRINI: More than that. At what point does one declare, "This is fascism and I must go to war against it?" And who does one war with? The whole apparatus of the country? If you are accused of being a traitor and you fight it—you defy it—does that turn you into a traitor? It does by their definition.

RADER: I am deeply afraid the country is headed for catastrophe.

PELLEGRINI: But under these present circumstances it's not clearly— it's tyranny, yes, but . . . one committee? An aberration? Or is this the real thing?

RADER: And the whole issue of self-preserv—

PELLEGRINI: —exactly. (*Beat*) Did you know I was a member of the Party for a while back in the thirties?

(RADER *and* PELLEGRINI *exit, lights out and up on* HEWITT *bedroom, baby still crying.*)

HEWITT: I'm gonna tell you something important—just once. And then I never want to talk about it again. When you were playin' hopscotch in front of your mama's stoop, I was telling Joe Stalin himself what I thought about his policy to the Negro race. I gave him a list of grievances and I told him to his face. You understand what I'm telling you. Right to his face.

ALETHIA: It doesn't matter now what you said to him, don't you understand? That's in the past. It's all talk!

HEWITT: Of course it's all talk, sweetheart! That's my point. It's all talk these days. Nobody gets shot, nobody disappears! What people *say* is all that matters—at least so far. We can move up and outta here if I play this right.

ALETHIA: All talk. I don't see us gettin' ahead. I see you all stressed all the time. You keep makin' promises and you go downtown. You keep goin' downtown. What do you do down there?

HEWITT: I sing for my supper. *Our* supper. It'll be all right.

ALETHIA (*to the baby*): I'm coming, I'm on my way. (*To him*) Don't take off without leaving me some money.

HEWITT: They are supposed to give me a voucher today. I only have subway fare and a little more for a doughnut. You don't have anything?

ALETHIA: That's what I'm saying. I'm completely broke. The kids need food. I need food.

HEWITT: I only got but twenty-five cents plus a nickel for the subway.

ALETHIA: Give me the quarter. (*Taking it and looking at it*) It ain't enough.

HEWITT: Give me a break.

ALETHIA: It ain't enough.

(*Lights out and up on* PELLEGRINI *and* RADER, *reentering.*)

PELLEGRINI: . . . I'm not sure. They were tossing around a lot of names.

RADER: A fishing expedition.

PELLEGRINI: I wanted to warn you. They seem especially interested in you.

RADER: I find that hard to believe. Me? Hmm. Were you . . . were you able to reassure them?

PELLEGRINI: I didn't say anything about anyone. I pleaded ignorance. Lack of memory. Don't worry about me saying anything damaging.

RADER: Damaging?

PELLEGRINI: That's what they're after. Betrayal. Divide and conquer. The usual fascist agenda. Here's my car. Want a ride?

RADER: No. I'll walk.

(PELLEGRINI *exits.* RADER *continues walking. Suddenly* JEWELL *and* HOUSTON *appear out of nowhere.*)

HOUSTON: Melvin Rader? (*Startled,* RADER *turns toward the sound. They look at each other.*)

(*Lights out and up on* HEWITT *and* ALETHIA.)

ALETHIA: . . . Ignorance! You got the choice of ignorance!

HEWITT: I gotta feed us and the kids.

ALETHIA: With blood money? I don't want it.

HEWITT: These people don't get called before these hearings for stealing candy! They're all guilty of something. I just supply some useful particulars to get the job done.

ALETHIA: It's under oath!

HEWITT: Get the baby will you. She's driving me crazy.

ALETHIA: She's hungry! She ain't got no food!

HEWITT: You gotta cut me some slack. Please. I know what I'm doin'. Take the baby carriage your mother gave you down to Lucky's Loan. You can borrow enough for today and I'll—

ALETHIA: —Mister stare-down-Joseph-Stalin is askin' his wife to sell the baby carriage.

HEWITT: Bullshit! This is for one day only! They're not getting me for free. We will have food and baby buggies and each other.

ALETHIA: Oh baby, don't you see? There'll be nothin' left of you.

You're for sale.

HEWITT: I am doing *business!* That's all. Why can't you see that? This is America. I gotta play by American rules. *It's what I have to do!* The Feds and the Reds are just two sides of the same coin. The difference is the Feds *need* me. And they *know* I know they need me. That's where I put a wedge. *You see?* They will give a little. That's the difference. That's what's keeping us alive.

ALETHIA: You're gonna be late.

HEWITT: No kiss for the old man?

ALETHIA (*going toward the crying baby*): Lucy needs me.

[LIGHTS OUT]

SUPERTITLE:

THEATRE OF CONJECTURE
Bouquets from the State Capitol
Seattle Repertory Playhouse
1948

The Seattle Repertory Playhouse. Present are FLORENCE BEAN JAMES, *seated apart,* ALBERT OTTENHEIMER, *a* STAGE MANAGER, *and other* ACTORS. *A rehearsal of the play* The Front Page *is in progress.*

SHERIFF: *Only you fellas got to lend a hand with us once in a while. We got a big job on our hands, smashing this Red menace—*

ENDICOTT: *—We gave you four columns yesterday. What do you want?*

SHERIFF: *That ain't it. The newspapers got to put their shoulders to the wheel. They've got to forcibly impress on the Bolsheviks that the death warrant for Earl Williams is a death warrant for every bomb-throwing un-American Red in this town. This hanging means more to the people of Chicago today. Now we're going to reform these Reds with a rope. That's our slogan. Quote me if you want to—*

STAGE MANAGER: Excuse me, Mr. Ottenheimer. You jumped into your next speech—

OTTENHEIMER (*Sheriff*): What? I did? Oh. I did, didn't I.

STAGE MANAGER: Yes. You're supposed to notice Murphy isn't listening to you, but reading the comics—

OTTENHEIMER: Oh yeah. Let's see . . .

MRS. JAMES (*coming forward*): While we're stopped. None of you seem to be responding to the circumstances of the scene. It's like you're at a garden— (HOUSTON *and* JEWELL *enter.*) Excuse me?

HOUSTON: We are looking for Mr. and Mrs. James.

MRS. JAMES: I am Mrs. James. You are interrupting our rehearsal.

HOUSTON: Is Mr. James around? And . . . uh, Albert Oppenheimer.

MRS. JAMES: It's *Ott*enheimer. Who are you?

HOUSTON: I am Investigator Houston from the Washington State Legislature. This is detective Jewell. Mr. Jewell?

JEWELL: This is a subpoena to appear before the Legislative Fact-Finding Committee—

OTTENHEIMER (*coming to them*): —What the hell is this?

JEWELL: You Ottenheimer? This is for you. It's official. It's a subpoena. To appear.

HOUSTON: Is Mr. James here?

OTTENHEIMER: He is not. He won't be in until tomorrow. Shall I give him something too?

HOUSTON: No. We'll come back. So you're rehearsing a play about Communists?

MRS. JAMES: No. *You're* rehearsing a play about Communists. Please leave the premises. We need to go back to work. (*She walks toward her chair.*) Places, everybody from the top of the scene.

(*By this time the program from the Playhouse's production of* The Front Page *is projected.*)

[LIGHTS FADE]

SUPERTITLE:

THEATRE OF RECORD

Herbert J. (Scoop) Phillips

Department of Philosophy, University of Washington

1948

PHILLIPS (*standing at a lectern*): I should like to emphasize that I am treating Marxism as a hypothesis. The assertion that the communist issue is *important* is not the assertion that the communist doctrine is *true*. One of the reasons so many informed people do not know what the Marxian philosophy is, is that it is generally regarded as a dangerous subject even to discuss. I believe there is considerable evidence that its *advocacy* is dangerous, but to admit that its *presentation* is dangerous implies that American history is considerably nearer a fascist stage than I am prepared to admit.

[BLACKOUT]

SUPERTITLE:

THEATRE OF RECORD

J. Edgar Hoover

FBI file

HOOVER: Subject Herbert Joseph Phillips is believed to be the leading member of the professional branch of the King County Communist Party, perhaps the most important Communist Party unit in the entire Northwest District. If not the most important branch, it most assuredly contains in its membership the most intelligent group of Communists in this area.

[BLACKOUT]

SUPERTITLE:

THEATRE OF RECORD

Member of Committee, Senator Thomas Bienz

Speech in Olympia, Washington

1948

BIENZ (*standing in light*): I regret that the committee cannot be given the right of summary executions.

[BLACKOUT]

SUPERTITLE:

THEATRE OF RECORD

Albert Canwell

Speech in Spokane, Washington

1947 or 1948

CANWELL: We cannot hang these people now, but when we get in the war with Russia we will be able to.

[BLACKOUT]

SUPERTITLE:

THEATRE OF CONJECTURE

Playing with Fire

The Washington Athletic Club

1948

A room in the hotel. CANWELL *answers the door,* VIOLA *enters.*

VIOLA: Hi, Mr. Canwell. I brought the empty file box you wanted.

CANWELL: Thank you, Mrs. Jaeger. The box doesn't matter. Put it down over there. Would you like a drink? Scotch?

VIOLA: Not really. Not now. Why isn't the box important? I thought . . . You were so insistent that I bring it to you at eight thirty.

CANWELL: And that's what it is—on the dot.

VIOLA (*pause*): I don't understand, Mr. Canwell.

CANWELL: I'll explain it all in good time. How about that drink? (*Goes to a table with one unopened bottle of scotch, a large bottle of club soda, ice, and two water glasses*) It's not often I get an opportunity—to ah, just get to know—uh—on a casual basis—or let us say it's not often I feel the—ah . . . responsibility to help someone . . . someone like yourself—to offer advice to someone who seems to be . . . ah . . . playing with fire.

VIOLA: Playing with fire?

CANWELL: Here. Let me fix you a . . . highball. Scotch! And would soda be all right?

VIOLA: Okay. You just bought this stuff, right?

CANWELL: That's right. Relax. Enjoy the view. It's a lovely evening, isn't it? Back home the stars will be as thick as fleas on a billy goat, ha, ha, ha. Where are you from, Mrs. Jaeger?

VIOLA: Me? Oh, I was born in Wisconsin but I moved here with my mother after my father got killed in the army. Where is your home?

CANWELL: Spokane. Where was your father killed? Europe or the Pacific?

VIOLA: Kansas. He was killed in Kansas, while training to be a soldier. I was only sixteen at the time, so my mother came here to work at Boeing's and I finished high school in—(*He hands her a drink.*) Thank you. This is starting to feel like a conversation you have when you're on a date.

CANWELL: Don't be silly, young lady.

VIOLA: I am realizing I'm in a hotel room with a man I hardly know.

CANWELL: Let's be clear, Mrs. Jaeger. I'm happily married, with a full load of principles. I am disciplined, to boot. I wouldn't invite you to my room if it were otherwise. I simply wanted to share my observations about you—to your face. I am a direct and frank man, Mrs. Jaeger.

VIOLA: Yes, sir. I see.

CANWELL (*lifting his glass*): Here's to America and all her beautiful children.

VIOLA: Here's to that. Okay. (*Pause*) What are we getting at here, Mr. Canwell?

CANWELL: Well, I've been thinking about the other evening at the newspaper offices. I worry that you being a beautiful woman— a divorcee—one who has experienced and suffered the end of a marriage—however brief and ill conceived it might have been.

VIOLA: What do you mean? You don't know anything about me.

CANWELL: I'm a very . . . *intuitive* sort of man, Mrs. Jaeger, and I deal on a regular basis with . . . compromised people, both men and women. (*He looks directly at her.*) I am familiar with the flaws of human nature. Most people I work with are neither traitors nor saints, but somewhere in the . . . murky *middle.* (*He smiles at her.*) But you see, Mrs. Jaeger . . . *if* . . . in this country there exists what I would call . . . an *aristocracy*—and I believe there is indeed a very real, if informal . . . *elite*—if we can call it that. And I think we can. If there is one, why then, I believe it consists of those few who have made choices in their lives to rise *above* the petty distractions of life. All for a higher purpose. So you see, Mrs. Jae—(*He has to clear his throat.*) I ask myself. If I react to some important issue in society that needs tending—lest we perish from the earth—and I commit to doing something about that—then how can I look at an *individual*—someone of your basic *caliber*—a person who appears to have a bit of *flint* between their . . . their what? . . . their *shoulder blades*—a little impertinent, perhaps—*feisty,* even. (*He laughs at this.*) Well. (*Pause, trying to be jovial*) I think a person of such qualities, and I include you as such a person—a person like that can—and *should*—be encouraged to seek a . . . I don't know . . . a higher *calling.*

VIOLA: I'm flattered you think so much of me, Mr. Canwell. You want me to join something? I don't understand.

CANWELL: That's not what I'm getting at.

VIOLA: What are you getting at? Are we going to keep standing here for so serious a conversation?

CANWELL: Oh, of course not. You sit in the chair. I'll sit here at the foot of the bed. The drink okay?

VIOLA: Yes, thank you. I still don't—

CANWELL: Can I get you another?

VIOLA: Not just yet, thank you. Aren't you going to have one?

CANWELL: No, I seldom drink. My church has a policy regarding drinking. This is soda.

VIOLA: Oh. Mormon?

CANWELL: Adventist.

VIOLA: What?

CANWELL: Seventh Day Adventist.

VIOLA: Oh. Never heard of it. Why are you offering me drinks, then? Why did you have me bring phony files to you?

CANWELL: Don't you worry about the scotch. And don't worry about *me*. (*Looking into her eyes*) You can rely on me to tell you what you need to know when you need to know it. And the files, my dear, were simply a ploy. After all, this is a hotel. No other motive.

VIOLA: Y'know, you say you're straightforward, but I don't know. I'm pretty confused.

CANWELL: I am as honest as an oak door. I am here with you because I recognize your promise and, frankly, I am worried about you.

VIOLA: What are you worried about me for?

CANWELL: You . . . you spent the other evening with three men. Four men. At the newspaper office. You drank whiskey with two of them. You're drinking with me in a hotel room. What does that make you, do you think?

VIOLA: Look, I can take care of myself. My old man is dead. I don't need . . . I'm an adult. I don't think I want to stay here any—

CANWELL: —You have been known to bring home men who you have just met. I know this for a fact. You look startled. My investigations cast as wide a net as I need them to. There was an occasion while you were still in high-school . . . your mother's friend? She worked at Boeing Aircraft too?

VIOLA (*standing*): How do you know this about me?

CANWELL: It was a small scandal. Certain teachers petitioned to have you expelled. (*Smiling warmly*) I am an investigator. I can find out just about anything I want to. Nobody else will learn of these things, you have my word.

VIOLA: I don't have to be here like this. I'm going.

CANWELL: Sit down, Mrs. Jaeger. I didn't bring you here to humiliate you. Quite the opposite. I'll pour you another drink.

VIOLA: I want to go home.

CANWELL: You're not tough enough for this, Mrs. Jaeger?

VIOLA: Yes, I'm tough enough. Anything I want to do, I'm tough enough for. I just don't want to be in a hotel room with a man I don't know who is accusing me of stuff that's none of his goddamn business. I don't care if you're Bishop Sheen, for Chrissake. You give me the willies. I'm leaving.

CANWELL: You sit down and listen to me right this minute or you won't have a job tomorrow morning, do you hear me? I won't tolerate this impertinence, you silly little . . . (*He stands up.*) Now cut it out! That's better. I am spending a great deal of time and effort away from my duties and thoughts of my family so that I can help you—

VIOLA: —Help me do what?

CANWELL: That's up to you. (*Pause*) I wouldn't presume to direct you in your life. This is a free country. A nation under God and therefore it's a country of second chances.

VIOLA: What am I supposed to do?

CANWELL: You tell me. You can figure it out. All I know is right now you're a swamp. You smell of corruption. You're . . . for the taking. Don't you see? I want to take you to higher ground, that's all. I believe in you.

VIOLA: I see. Well, Mr. Canwell, I don't want you to take me anywhere. I . . . I want you to . . . Who do you think you are? You have no right . . . you pried into my private life. (*She raises her voice.*) Who do you think you are?!

CANWELL: Your friend.

VIOLA: My friend? You know what? I'll tell you what. Shove it, mister! Just shove it!

(VIOLA *turns to the door and exits.* CANWELL *stands stock still.*)

[LIGHTS FADE]

SUPERTITLE:

THEATRE OF RECORD

President Allen Addresses the Faculty

1948

ALLEN: We at the university must maintain our unity and dignity. We cannot afford to engage in a public fight with the Canwell committee. My reconnaissance of the situation shows me that the climate of public opinion is strongly running against radicalism and is currently being conditioned against allowing proved Communists to hold public employment. I doubt the Board of Regents will defend individuals found to be engaged in secret activities of dubious character.

[BLACKOUT]

SUPERTITLE:

THEATRE OF RECORD

University of Washington Student

1948

STUDENT: I came all the way from Philadelphia to attend the university. Nobody ever told me it was a communistic university.

[BLACKOUT]

SUPERTITLE:

THEATRE OF CONJECTURE

Joe and Joey Receive a Caller

1948

A small portion of the Butterworth apartment. A table is cluttered with books, unwashed dishes, pots and pans, full ashtrays, scattered mail. Near the table on the floor are stacks of books, old newspapers, clothing. There is a console radio. Claustrophobic and chaotic. JOE BUTTERWORTH *is sitting at the table, reading a book, and eating out of a pan. Nearby,* JOEY, *his son, is sitting/lying/ slumping in an easy chair concentrating on untangling the string of a yo-yo. Tableaux. Silence. A loud door buzzer sounds.*

JOEY: I'll get it! (*Running to offstage door*) Who's there? Oh, I know you!
WINTHER (*off*): Hi . . . Joey? Your father in?
JOEY: Daddy, a teacher from—a teacher from . . . from the un-ivers-ity. Who're you? I forgot.
WINTHER: I'm Sophus. Dr. Winther. I work with your father.
JOEY (*too loud*): Your friend the doctor Winter!
WINTHER (*he enters, humoring* JOEY): Win*th*er, not winter.
JOEY (*teasing*): Old Man Winter! Daddy! Old Man Winter is calling on you! (*He laughs at his joke.*)
BUTTERWORTH (*standing, taking his napkin from his front, and wiping his mouth*): Sophus, come in. Uh . . . excuse the clutter . . .

WINTHER (*looking around*): My God, man, this is . . . you ought to . . . uh . . . to get someone *in* here. This is . . . I guess Dorothy was the housekeeper in the family—

JOEY: —Dorothy is dead. Did you know that, mister? We are . . . "fending for ourselves." (*He laughs.*)

BUTTERWORTH: Quiet down, Joey! Here, Sophus . . . (*Removing clutter from a wooden chair and offering it to* WINTHER, *who continues to absorb the chaos of the apartment*) To what do we owe the honor of your uh . . . can I guess?

WINTHER: The boy? We need to talk.

JOEY (*handing* WINTHER *his yo-yo*): Fix my yo-yo, will you, Mister? The string is tw-is-ted. It don't work.

BUTTERWORTH: *Doesn't* work.

JOEY: "Doesn't." Fix it?

BUTTERWORTH: You have to leave us alone, Joey. Turn on the radio. Quietly. Sophus and I need to—

JOEY: —The *radio!* (JOEY *goes to the console radio and turns it on. It takes a few minutes to warm up and when it does it is too loud.*)

BUTTERWORTH: A drink? All I've got is bourbon. Neat.

WINTHER: No. No thank you. (BUTTERWORTH *drinks throughout scene.*) Can you and I, perhaps, go to some other location? I don't want to bother the boy—

BUTTERWORTH: —Naw. Joey's . . . uh—I don't want to leave him—

WINTHER: —You can't call a baby-sitter? We need to talk—

(*The radio has warmed up.*)

BUTTERWORTH: So *talk,* for Chrissake. Joey turn the radio down! (*The sound of the radio show* Fibber McGee and Molly, *just barely audible, plays under scene.*) Talk. You came here to . . . the committee, right?

WINTHER: Yes, of course— (*Absentmindedly trying to untangle the yo-yo string)*

BUTTERWORTH: —They're goons, Sophus. Relax. Don't talk to them. Today—I talked too much, today. I blew my stack. They're not worth the time of day—

WINTHER: —We can't ignore them, Joe. They've been to visit me. They know most everything. They have us dead to rights. What they don't know they're figuring out.

BUTTERWORTH: They're making accusations. They'll say anything to rattle you.

WINTHER: They know where we had meetings, when we met, with whom we met. They have been thorough. I wrote an anonymous article years ago for *Harper's Weekly* describing why I left the Party. My *wife* doesn't know I wrote it. They do. Everybody is informing on everybody else.

(Pause)

JOEY *(laughing)*: Fibber McGee opened the closet! Daddy, he opened the closet!

BUTTERWORTH: Yes, boy—

JOEY: —It's so funny, Daddy, when he opens the door—every time—

BUTTERWORTH: —Yes, boy—

WINTHER: —But here's the thing, Joe. There is no *harm,* see? If everyone tells on everyone else and it all becomes public— then there is no conspiracy, don't you see? That's how we neutralize the impact of the committee. We apologize and get on with our lives. Nobody goes to jail, no one gets fired. And if everyone agrees—then no one loses friends or colleagues. It's simple. It's a formality. A sincere formality. Otherwise, this is very serious, Joe. There is really no choice, no other option.

BUTTERWORTH: What if I'm still in the Party?

WINTHER: Oh my God, I was afraid of this. (*Pause*) Then you're a damn fool. I thought you would have advanced beyond that tired, corrupt—

BUTTERWORTH: —I see. Why did you bother to come see me?

WINTHER: Because I don't like waste. I don't like mess. Joe, don't be a fool—

BUTTERWORTH: —Let's leave me out of this for a moment. Let's assume that some of our friends and colleagues are still in the Party and might choose prison, exile, or even death before capitulating in the manner you are suggesting. (*Pause*) Are you running around attempting to make last-minute changes in other people's *character*? *Sophus!* Who are you trying to kid here?

WINTHER: Those who refuse to go along will be left to their own devices. I'm sorry, but if they lack the perspective to see beyond—we can't be responsible for—

BUTTERWORTH: —Sophus, my dear old—you are not going to become a Judas, now, are you? No, no, no. If you were to betray your fellows, you'd have to swallow—you'd spend the rest of your life trying to justify it to yourself. And you'd fail. Don't Sophus, don't.

WINTHER: This is a plague and if we don't help cure it, we will perish of it. There is no middle ground. I've never been so sure of anything in my life.

BUTTERWORTH: I remember a time when you were very *sure* the masses of poor and starving working people needed to control their destiny, and you were sure we as intellectuals had a responsibility to help give that to them.

WINTHER: You're speaking antiquated rot—

BUTTERWORTH: —I was there when you made a pledge to put

yourself on the line for the dignity of humanity *in-the-abstract!* You vowed to fight for the future of *strangers.* And now you're willing to put the future of those you *know* on the line—your friends and coworkers—to keep your ass out of the fire. My God—

WINTHER: —You'll lose your position, Joe. Don't you understand? One way or the other, unless you go along with this, you will no longer teach at the university. Since Dorothy passed on—

BUTTERWORTH: —She killed herself. Let's not mince words.

JOEY (*from beside the radio*): Dorothy killed herself! She used a rope—

WINTHER: —I am not mincing words, for God's sake! I'm trying to show respect! Since she . . . killed herself, your performance here at the university has been suffering. President Allen has been made aware you only have two graduate students. And that they are unhappy with your lack of focus. There are rumors of a drinking problem. He's willing to bend over backwards in return for your full cooperation. He won't settle for anything less—there will be no compromise on that. He'll tell you all this himself—

BUTTERWORTH: —You're terrified, aren't you?

WINTHER: Dr. Allen sent me a memo this afternoon. You are to make an appointment with him tomorrow.

BUTTERWORTH: I have other plans.

WINTHER: This is official now. Professor Butterworth, I *demand* you cooperate with the policy of this University. (*Pause*) I know you. My God, Joe. (*Pause*) You are a lot of things but I wouldn't have taken you for a fool. You are too intelligent and too experienced to be hoodwinked by martyrdom.

BUTTERWORTH: "And thus with fayned flaterye and japes, He made the persoun and the peple his apes." Not so with me. I decline your offer to have me participate with you in your betrayal of me. Go away.

WINTHER (*pause*): Well then, goodbye Joe. (*He rises.*) Here, Joey. I untangled the string. It should work now.

(WINTHER *exits;* JOEY *approaches.*)

JOEY (*speaking slowly and accurately*): See? He fixed the twisted string.

[LIGHTS FADE]

[END OF ACT ONE]

Act 2, "The Long-Wave End of the Spectrum": Marin Perry (Mrs. Phillips), Joel McHale (Caughlan), Barry Hubbard (Henry), Lori Larsen (Mrs. James), Bruno Oliver (O'Brien), and J.R. Drew (Gundlach).

ACT TWO

SUPERTITLE:

THEATRE OF CONJECTURE
The Long-Wave End of the Spectrum
Seattle Repertory Playhouse
1948

Present are FLORENCE JAMES, BURTON JAMES, ALBERT OTTEN-
HEIMER, TED ASTLEY, RALPH GUNDLACH, JOE BUTTERWORTH,
MRS. HELGA PHILLIPS, HAROLD EBY, GARLAND ETHEL, MELVILLE
JACOBS, MELVIN RADER, ANGELO PELLEGRINI—*all subpoenaed.*
Also present are attorneys JOHN CAUGHLAN, CLIFFORD O'BRIEN,
and ED HENRY. *It is night.*

MRS. JAMES: I'll bring this meeting to order. Thank you all for
coming. I seem to be the speechmaker in the family, so I vol-
unteered to run this get-together. Thank you all for coming.
(*She looks them over.*) This is some rogue's gallery we have here.
Some of us are friends, some former friends, political allies,
former political allies, husbands and wives, *former* husbands
and wives, and all the rest I won't even go into. (*There is laughter.*) All of us in this room except for the three lawyers lurking
off to the side there have been subpoenaed. John Caughlan,

Clifford O'Brien, and Ed Henry either represent you already or are available to do so. There seem to be very few attorneys who are willing to soil their reputations by associating with us. We are fortunate because these three are, by all accounts, excellent attorneys as well as friends to us and our cause.

PELLEGRINI: Whose cause is that, Mrs. James? My cause?

MRS. JAMES: Please be patient. Everyone will have the opportunity to speak his mind. Please hear me out.

PELLEGRINI: I get very nervous—you start talking about "causes" I am not a part of.

OTTENHEIMER: "It is the cause, it is the cause, my soul, let me not name it to you . . ." You can relax, sir, no one is trying to hoodwink anyone here.

MRS. JAMES: Let me back up a moment. We called this meeting because we thought it important to try to come to some unified response to this . . . outrage—I don't know what else to call it. We are all under siege. Are we not? Isn't this indisputable? I think it's only prudent that we talk this out with one another. Now, I know we don't all agree about a lot of things—some of us have vastly different political ideas and agendas—but I am hoping that we can arrive at a single response to the committee's actions—that we will . . . that we'll all agree to defy the committee—

RADER: —Excuse me, if I may, Mrs. James.

MRS. JAMES: Yes, Mel. I am opening this up for discussion now. This is Melvin Rader of the Philosophy Department.

RADER: I don't think, on the face of it, that you—or anyone—can expect unanimity on this matter. Each individual will have to follow his conscience. Our individual sense of honor as well as each of our livelihoods are at stake—

MRS. PHILLIPS: —This is precisely why we have to *achieve* unanimity. Excuse me. I'm Helga, Scoop Phillips' wife—

MRS. JAMES: —Please wait your turn—

MRS. PHILLIPS: —He's in New York this summer, teaching at Columbia. We have been subpoenaed along with the rest of you. He is planning on *not coming back*. He is planning on defying the committee. You know why? Because if we don't all rise above saving our individual butts, as it were, the committee will make hash of us. Only if we achieve a solidarity—

PELLEGRINI: You're talking the Party line, Helga. You're trying to get us all to fall into some line or—we are not a flock of ducks in a row!

MRS. JAMES: Please everyone! If we get into a shouting match nothing will be accomplished—

MRS. PHILLIPS (*ignoring* MRS. JAMES): —My husband is an open Marxist. He's got nothing to hide—he never has—but he's damned if he's going to tell those s.o.b.'s that—*even though it will mean his job!* That's what I'm saying here. It's a simple black and white issue. Do you stand for justice or don't you? Are we going to take the initiative or are we going to let this goddamned—this *fascist* committee define the argument here? Is that what you are going to allow, Pelli?

EBY: They have already defined it, Helga—

MRS. JAMES: —Please, please, everyone. We mustn't let this descend into accusations and personal challenges. I will recognize each person who wants to speak, in turn. Angelo Pellegrini—from the English Department. Do you want to have your say?

PELLEGRINI: It makes my skull ache to be here even *listening* to this. A decade ago it was the same song—this "solidarity." It's old hat. It's dumb. It's fallacious. I have my own beliefs, and they happen to include a responsibility of looking out for the welfare and future of my family—

MRS. PHILLIPS: —Oh, for God's sake—

PELLEGRINI: —My honor is a matter for me to sort out! With myself—

MRS. PHILLIPS: —Scoop and I have three children. That doesn't absolve us of responsibility to—

PELLEGRINI: —I will not allow my honor to go on trial here! It is accountable to no one in this room! I want all of you to understand that. You will not make me into a cog on someone else's wheel. *Non mollare!* No doing. I said good-bye to all this years ago. Good night.

(PELLEGRINI *exits.*)

MRS. JAMES (*after a beat*): Dr. Rader?

RADER: I am afraid I agree with him and will have to dismiss myself from this discussion. It would be counter to everything I stand for to restrict myself—to do other than answer candidly—to not respond to any . . . to my accusers. And until it is decided in a court of law to be otherwise, as odious as it might be, there is no other path for me to take but to present myself and my positions as clearly . . . as clearly as possible to any authoritative body who asks me. That is *my* position only. I judge no one else's actions here. (*There is a moment of silence.*) I have no doubt of your sincerity and well meaning—

BUTTERWORTH: Please don't condescend, Mel, we are not a bunch of machinated puppets, regardless of how convenient it is for you to view us thus.

RADER: I don't mean to. I simply cannot turn my volition over to a group. Any group. I am sorry.

ASTLEY: You're turning it over to *them,* is what you're doing. You know, it's you liberals that defeat real progress—

MRS. JAMES: —Ted, we are going to keep this civil—

ASTLEY: Fascists, at least, let you know where they stand. It's you guys who want it both ways that drive me—

MRS. JAMES: I insist on order here!

RADER: I wish us all the best of luck. Good night.

(RADER *exits*.)

MRS. JAMES: Ted, I will ask you not to speak again tonight.

ASTLEY: I will do my best.

MRS. JAMES: Can the rest of us arrive at a consensus? We can still provide a powerful front.

(*A beat of silence*.)

GUNDLACH: Well, I've come around to not cooperating—to boy-cotting the whole thing. A week ago I felt differently. I like my job very much. It's been an arduous journey for me since this all began, with a lot of pain—and I think it will continue to be. I don't want to lose my job. And I don't want to go to jail. But we have to fight this. We have to stop these buggers in their tracks or we'll have a real mess in this country. You can count me in.

MRS. JAMES: Wonderful, Ralph. This is Ralph Gundlach, every-body. He's president of the Western Psychological Association. Dr. Jacobs has the floor.

JACOBS: I have to tell you that I am terrified and I see no way out of this. I haven't been actively "political" for some—since the Hitler-Stalin pact. All that I do as an anthropologist has been, however, informed by many influences, including the man of the hour here, Karl Marx.

MRS. PHILLIPS: The pact was a necessary tactic to keep Germany from invading—

JACOBS: —Please let me finish. Please! I was also very much

influenced by the anthropologist Boas. I studied under him. But have parted company with *him too* in large and significant ways. I doubt I will ever be held accountable for my embrace of and then my pulling away from the great Boas. But I have been subpoenaed. That means I am going to be asked, in public, to explain my relationship to Marx. I'd rather not. But I want you to know I am willing to do that. I will because the alternative would not only mean throwing away this particular position at the university, it means that without such a position I could not practice my profession at all. If I am fired, not only will I lose my only means of support but I will be emasculated professionally. Anthropology is what I do. It is who I am. My relationship to Marx is mostly in the past—it is a footnote to who I am and to what I do. My relationship to the Party is now nonexistent. I may still lose my job, but I am not going to throw it away in the name of a political battle that I haven't chosen. What lies ahead for me is worrisome. I haven't had a decent night's sleep in nearly a month. But this is my position: I will try to keep my job—and at the same time serve my conscience. That is my dilemma. And it is, first, a *personal* dilemma. Whether it is a social dilemma has become only a matter of abstract speculation, and for others to judge. Not so, my personal crisis. I wonder, Mrs. James. It seems we are in similar straits. How will you be able to ply your trade without an audience?

MRS. JAMES: There are certain depths to which I will not descend, no matter the consequences. Harold Eby? Do you want to speak?

EBY: I think Dr. Jacobs speaks for me. I will not name names. I promise you that.

MRS. JAMES: Garland Ethel?

ETHEL: No names. That's all I promise.

MRS. JAMES: Joe Butterworth?

BUTTERWORTH: I will not attend.

MRS. PHILLIPS: Scoop told me to tell you he will be unavailable for the hearings.

MRS. JAMES: Ted Astley?

ASTLEY: I think I'll stay at home, read a book.

MRS. JAMES: Burton?

BURTON: I will not go.

OTTENHEIMER: I always did go with the crowd . . . er that is—*stay* with the crowd. (*Beat*) God I hate this.

CAUGHLAN: If you'll permit me, everyone. I'm John Caughlan, attorney for several of you. But I want to speak as an observer of history, not as a lawyer. (*Beat*) Every act is a political act as well as what else it might be, and every *relationship* is a political relationship as well as what else it might contain. From the most intimate to the most public. In husband and wife relationships, employer-employee relationships, in merchant-consumer relationships, and in the relationship between a subpoenaed citizen and a legislative committee. In the most private as well as the most public activities there is always a political struggle occurring—a struggle, at least a negotiation, for—*power.* The question at hand is whether, during the hearings, each of you chooses to embrace or chooses to ignore this sometimes open, sometimes hidden fact. To ignore this reality is at best, naive—and at worst, pure folly. I believe the other side understands this better than we do. They have reinvented an age-old game in which the main rule is: you are guilty unless you renounce your thoughts, your beliefs—and the company you keep. They understand the nature and use of power. They understand this better than we do at the moment. This is our weakness—a deficiency we in this room all seem to share. Regardless of what Pellegrini says, there is already, by default, a solidarity here among all of you who are subpoenaed—the solidarity of *victimhood.* That is the nature of your solidarity. Unless you turn it into something else.

MRS. JAMES: Do you have a suggestion?

CAUGHLAN: Yes. First, I think that those who are not ready to defy the committee should leave now. I am about to declare attorney-client relationship privileges.

HENRY: Then I, too, advise all of you who do *not* intend to break the law by defying the committee at the outset leave this meeting immediately with me. Good night and good luck, everyone. (EBY, JACOBS, *and* ETHEL *exit with* HENRY.)

CAUGHLAN: Okay. From this moment on everything we do is going to be a very dicey situation, legally speaking.

OTTENHEIMER: Why is that?

O'BRIEN: Remember the Spanish Inquisition?

OTTENHEIMER: Slightly before my time.

O'BRIEN: Well, you'll get to catch it this time around. Now, as your attorneys we need to point out that you all face almost certain contempt charges which will subject each of you to jail sentences of up to a year and fines of up to a thousand dollars. So you must be sure you are willing to face these very real consequences. Anyone want to reconsider? (*Silence*) All right. Now here is where it gets a bit complicated. John? This was your idea.

CAUGHLAN: In order to protect the attorney-client relationship of privacy we have to . . . we need to divide the tasks of representing you. How about I take on Mrs. James, Ted, and Scoop Phillips, and Mr. O'Brien here will represent Al, Joe, Burton, and Ralph. Agreed? Okay. Now I speak to those who I am representing. As your attorney, I must emphasize your legal culpability for defying the wishes of a lawful committee. Is that clear?

GUNDLACH: It's clear to me.

CAUGHLAN: Any questions? All right. To you others I now speak as your friend and compatriot. Sorry, Mrs. James, Ted, I am not speaking to you now. You are simply overhearing an informal conversation with my friends. Friends: if you want to challenge the committee's validity at every turn, I recommend the following. First, you announce publicly and loudly that you have no intention of even showing up—that you won't cooperate at all—that you will not acknowledge the existence of the committee as a valid and legal entity. In the meantime, O'Brien and I will ask the court for restraining orders and initiate court challenges against the whole premise of the committee. You will need to get a defense committee started, petitions signed, gather as much public support as possible. Then if the hearings do proceed, when they get under way I suggest you *do* show up. You appear at the last minute, quote, "under duress." We should organize ongoing picket lines who will protest at the armory all during the hearings. Together our task, in the political sense, will be to convince the public that it is these *hearings* which are un-American. We will fight it out legally, politically, and materially—in the hearing room, under their spotlights—right in their faces. We will attempt to turn their force back on themselves, coolly, efficiently, and in the moment of conflict. That, in my opinion, is the honorable way to proceed. Clifford, would you like to say anything to my clients?

O'BRIEN: Sure. (*Pause*) Ditto!

CAUGHLAN: Well put, counselor.

[LIGHTS OUT]

SUPERTITLE:

THEATRE OF CONJECTURE
Absolution
1948

CANWELL'S *room at the Athletic Club. Again,* CANWELL *answers the door and* VIOLA *stands there.*

CANWELL: Yes? Hmmph. This is not appropriate. I have nothing to say to you.

VIOLA: Can I come in?

CANWELL: Not appropriate. You go on your way, Mrs.—

VIOLA: —I don't have a job. I went to work this morning and I don't have a job—

CANWELL: —You just be on your way. I know nothing—

VIOLA: —You got me *fired!* You can't do—please let me come in?

CANWELL: This is all your affair. I am not going to talk to someone else's former employee about their problems. There are proper channels I'm sure—

VIOLA: —Please don't do this to me. Let me talk to you just for a minute. We can work this out. Please.

(*He pauses, opens door wider; she passes in.*)

CANWELL: I won't tolerate any nonsense. I won't hesitate to call the front desk if you—

VIOLA: —I won't make a scene. I just want my job back.

CANWELL: I am not the person to talk to about that.

VIOLA: Yes you are. Mr. Niendorff told me that I no longer meet standards—that there are questions of my character and reliability. I have been a good secretary, a good worker. (*She begins crying.*) What did you tell him about me?

CANWELL: There is nothing for you to take personally. You'll find another job, I'm sure.

VIOLA: I don't want another job. Look, Mr. Canwell, I am really sorry for what I said. Couldn't I do something to prove I don't have—what was the word Mr. Niendorff used?—moral turpitude? I don't have that. I'm a good person.

CANWELL: We are not talking about "good" and "bad." I misjudged you. It's all right. I'm sure you'll do fine. I don't have time—

VIOLA: —*Please!* Just tell me what you want—

CANWELL: You see? You don't understand. I don't want anything from you. I was only interested—the reason I brought you here in the first place was—I wanted to help you achieve something you've probably only glimpsed—

VIOLA: I want to be more, Mr. Canwell. I want to be—I can be. You can help me. I'd be honored if you'd try to help me . . .

CANWELL (*pause, he assesses*): I'm curious.

VIOLA: What?

CANWELL: What did you tell them down at the desk?

VIOLA: I didn't want to make anything awkward for you. I just walked on the elevator. It was open. I pretended I belong here.

CANWELL: This is not a cat and mouse game, Mrs. Jaeger. I had no intention of ever—I frankly never thought I'd—I'd see or interact with you again. Is that clear?

VIOLA: Oh. Yes. No. I . . . what do you mean? Oh. That I would figure in order to get my job back you'd expect me to show up . . . ? Oh, no.

CANWELL: Frankly I don't have time for any of this. Any of . . . I've got a lot of work ahead of—

VIOLA: —I don't want to interfere—

CANWELL: —Are you capable of being vulnerable before the Lord? Can you come unto Him as a child?

VIOLA: I don't know. I think . . . I can try.

CANWELL: And are you tough, as you claimed? Can you suffer?

VIOLA: If I have to.

CANWELL: It's for you.

VIOLA: The suffering?

CANWELL: Yes. All of it. I don't know if this is right—

VIOLA: Let's go.

CANWELL: This is awkward—uh . . . (*A long pause*) Give me your hand. Viola. (*Pause*) I am going to call you Viola from now on because that's the name Christ knows you by. The One who knows you inside and out.

VIOLA: I'm a little scared, Mr.—

CANWELL: —Of course, of course. That's only natural. But you will become glorious. You will become invincible. You simply have to pay the price, that's all. I wish . . . I wish I weren't the one—

VIOLA: What do I have to pay?

CANWELL: You have to pay Christ. You have to give Him your sins. Isn't it amazing? The only payment He asks are your sins. Then you make a pact with Him to follow His Word faithfully. And when you do this, you will have a clean slate and everlasting life. It is so utterly glorious, do you see? Do you want to have a conversation with Him?

VIOLA: You mean a confession?

CANWELL: Yes. You are asked to confess and atone for your sins. That's the beginning and the end. You feel my hand, right?

VIOLA: Yes.

CANWELL: It's firm, right?

CANWELL: It's gentle though too, right?

VIOLA: Uh huh.

CANWELL: Just remember that. My hand is full of love.

VIOLA: Okay. What are you going to do?

CANWELL: Do you give your sins to the Lord Jesus Christ?

VIOLA: I . . . (*Pause*) I . . . do. Yes. He can take my sins.

CANWELL: Talk directly to Him, Viola. He hears you, He sees you, His arms are open for your sins.

VIOLA: Oh. (*Pause*) Oh. (*A beat*) Yes. (*Looking out*) Dear . . . Jesus . . . take (*Beginning to break down*) take . . . my sins. (*Pause*) Take . . . my . . . ssss . . . oh me (*Pause*) . . . yes. Thank you. Thank you, Mr. Canwell. (*She leans into him.*)

CANWELL (*pause*): What are they?

VIOLA: What?

CANWELL: What are your sins?

VIOLA: Oh. (*Pause*) Well. Uh . . . well, I just kind of gave them all away, I didn't enumerate—

CANWELL: —But you must.

VIOLA: Well, I have so many. (*She laughs.*) Do we have all night?

CANWELL: You know what I mean.

VIOLA: You want me to humiliate myself? I should mention them?

CANWELL: Not for me. For Him. Trust me.

VIOLA: Well, I've done so much, where to begin . . . ?

CANWELL: The men . . .

VIOLA: The men? Oh. Oh, god . . . (*Pause*) well . . . he wants me to tell Him I've slept with several men?

CANWELL: I don't think Jesus wants you to pretty up your sins. You know what a euphemism is?

VIOLA: Of course. I work in a newspaper office.

CANWELL: All right. In the face of God you don't have to mince words. (*Slight pause*) You have had sexual intercourse—isn't that what it's called? Sometimes with strangers? Tell Jesus that.

VIOLA: All right. I had sexual . . . this is hard. I have had sexual intercourse with men—

CANWELL: You allowed your vagina to be penetrated—

VIOLA: Please—please don't—

CANWELL: —to be slathered with semen—like a cow in heat lets any old bull into her, didn't you? You were no better than an animal in the eyes of our Lord were you?

VIOLA: I . . . I . . . you make it sound worse . . .

CANWELL: You let another *woman*—

VIOLA: —I was a girl . . . I didn't . . .

CANWELL: You let another woman put herself on you . . . and I don't know what else . . . You touched and kissed and whatever until God's gift shuddered within you—stolen from heaven like a jackal stealing a lamb. You are filth. (*Slight pause, she starts to pull away.*) But Jesus is love. He will take your filth with open arms.

VIOLA: Oh my god . . . I don't get this . . . I'm not sure . . . (*She is sobbing.*)

CANWELL: You want to feel clean again, Viola? You feel the love and firmness in my hand?

VIOLA: Yes. Yes.

CANWELL: Well talk to Him. I am not Jesus. I am of the earth.

VIOLA: Jesus . . . ? I . . . Jesus take my sins . . . my pain . . . (*Pause*) . . . I feel so . . . I feel so bad . . .

CANWELL: Don't you feel Jesus' love? He's here with you. Don't you feel it?

VIOLA (*after a moment*): I do . . . you know . . . ? I do . . .

CANWELL: You do? Well you see how simple it is. Isn't it glorious? Now I will take your pain away here on earth. But I will have to cause another kind of pain. Do you know what I mean?

VIOLA: No.

CANWELL: No, maybe you don't. I will help . . . I feel such sweet compassion for you. You lost your father—you lost his guidance just when you needed it. What would he have done if he had known of your badness? You have been bad. Your father was off defending the country and couldn't look after you. What would he have done?

VIOLA: I don't know. He wasn't all that . . .

CANWELL: I think I know what he would have done. If he was a good and loving man to his daughter, I know what he would have done.

VIOLA: What would he have done . . .?

CANWELL: He would have . . . he would have taken you behind the barn.

VIOLA: The what?

CANWELL: It's a figure of speech, in this instance. You will feel purged and cleansed here on earth. You will become part of the family of Christ as well.

VIOLA: I am scared and I feel sick to my . . .

CANWELL: But you're tough. Remember?

VIOLA: What are you going to do to me?

CANWELL: The anticipation is worse than the beating itself. I am going to do what your father would have done out of love and concern. Now turn around. Let go my hand. My loving hand. I am only helping cleanse you. Let go my hand and turn around. That's better. (*She kneels down, looking up at him.*) No. Get off your knees. That's right. It's going to make it all go away. Grab hold of your ankles.

VIOLA: No.

CANWELL: Show me some strength of character, Viola. You have what it takes. Show me some flint.

VIOLA: Please don't kill me.

CANWELL: Oh, dear, dear Viola. Nobody is going to kill you. You are graced by Jesus. Don't cry. I won't lead you astray. That's better. Hold your ankles.

VIOLA: No.

CANWELL: Hold your ankles.

VIOLA: Please. I don't want to.

CANWELL: Hold them. Now. (*Pause*) There. Be strong in this and you will be strong in everything. You will be glorious. (*He takes off his belt as . . .*)

[LIGHTS FADE]

SUPERTITLE:
THEATRE OF RECORD
Albert Canwell
1995

CANWELL: I don't have—this may sound like a racist remark— but I don't have the greatest confidence in most Negroes. In the Party they'd pick them out, carry along, bed them down with a white girl, whatever was necessary to get them active in the Party. But they'd never make good Communists because they're not intellectual in general unless—oh here and there you find one like oh—trying to think of one we had as a witness. But they're not too dependable or reliable, so without making any issue of it, you don't lean on them much. It's just a waste of time.

[BLACKOUT]

SUPERTITLE:
THEATRE OF CONJECTURE
The Orientation
July 1948

The Armory Building in Seattle. The committee's offices. CANWELL, NIENDORFF, *and* HOUSTON *sitting.* HEWITT *and* ASHLEY *enter.*

ASHLEY: Gentlemen: George Hewitt.

CANWELL (*standing and shaking hands*): Mr. Hewitt, Al Canwell, chairman of the committee. My chief investigator, Bill Houston. Uh, Fred here is from one of the local papers. He just wants to meet you. This is strictly off the record. He will shortly leave us. Oh. And this is our secretary, Mrs. Jaeger.

HEWITT: How do you do?

HOUSTON: We've heard a lot about you, George . . .

HEWITT: You can call me Mr. Hewitt. And I'll call you Mr. . . . ?

HOUSTON: Houston. William Houston.

HEWITT: Yes. I'd like to keep things formal and aboveboard.

HOUSTON: Oh sure, that's fine. Any way you want it.

CANWELL: Out here in the West, we tend to be a bit more informal than back . . . uh . . . No offense meant, I'm sure.

HEWITT: And none taken, I'm sure. I . . . ah . . . I'm not accustomed to newspapermen participating in my functions as a witness. I'd like him to . . .

NIENDORFF: Hey, relax, fella—er . . . Mr. Hewitt. We are on your side.

HEWITT: My side? How do you know *my* side? I'm supposed to be an objective witness, aren't I? What side are you talking about?

NIENDORFF: That's right. We all are. Objective. That's the credo of my business. The facts. But we do have opinions. Of course we save 'em for our editorial—

HEWITT: —I'm getting uncomfortable, General.

ASHLEY: Mr. Hewitt's had a long aeroplane ride from New York City. Sit down, Mr. Hewitt.

HEWITT: No thanks. I've been sitting for a long time . . . (*Pause, everyone sizing each other up*) How long do you expect this to take?

ASHLEY: He's been pulled away from his family, didn't even get to say good-bye. Just made the plane. You know . . . ah, Mr.

Hewitt's about to be a father for the what . . . the third time?

HOUSTON: Well, congratulations . . .

CANWELL: That's mighty fine. I've got six myself—

HEWITT: —Let's cut the crap, what do you say, eh?

CANWELL: Now there's no need—

HEWITT: —Get the newspaper guy out of here so we can get orientated about what's gonna happen so I can check into a hotel.

CANWELL: Fine, fine. Fred just wanted to meet you face-to-face. Don't worry about him. He is the soul of discretion.

HEWITT: Really.

CANWELL: Mrs. Jaeger, where is Mr. Hewitt staying while he is our guest? At the Roosevelt?

VIOLA: The Roosevelt? Well, uh . . . no, actually they were full, I think. Fred suggested I call another one. The . . . Moore Hotel.

ASHLEY: See you later, Fred.

NIENDORFF: Right. Good-bye, Mr. Hewitt nice to meet you. That spelled with two "t's"?

HEWITT: Hmm hm.

(NIENDORFF *exits*.)

ASHLEY: Let's get down to it. A chair . . . (HEWITT *shakes his head no*.)

HOUSTON: Okay. Tell us about this . . . what's it called? Briehl's farm? Some kinda school for Commies?

HEWITT: Before we begin our . . . relationship here, there are a few things I want to get clear.

CANWELL: What's on your mind?

HEWITT: I don't know if you all can appreciate the fact that what I do these days . . . I have a particular . . . and, I am quite sure, a *temporary* usefulness to certain parties . . . ah . . . certain—

CANWELL: —Not too much use to the *Communist* Party these days, though, ha, ha, ha . . . But go on.

ASHLEY: What are you getting at, Hewitt?

HEWITT: I'll tell you. I'll tell you. The young lady may want to excuse herself because I'm gonna talk frank—man to man. Understand?

CANWELL: Mrs. Jaeger will stay in the room—

ASHLEY: —If he would find himself more at ease by having the lady—

CANWELL: She will not leave the room until I say so! Is that clear? We are not intimidated!

HEWITT: I don't expect you are.

VIOLA: Thank you, Mr. Canwell.

HEWITT: But I haven't got a lot of patience with people trying to jerk me . . . I got no time to talk no talk without some clear *agreement* on the subject of how we compensate one another. Understand? Now, I want to introduce you people to a few ground rules—to the basic shit of what goes down. In other words, you want me in your game—here's what happens. First, I want a nice—a *decent*—room in this *Roosevelt Hotel*—the one that's full up. It sounds like they don't want *this* nigger in the beds they rent, that means they don't want *any* black folks between their sheets. Well today, you people are going to change that policy—at least while I am residing in your city. Furthermore, I will want to eat in their dining room, if I so choose. And that brings me to how we *pay* for the board. You see, my memory can get pretty rusty about stuff that white folks did with one another, eight or ten years ago—like I really give a shit. You follow what I'm sayin'? Now what seems to . . . ah . . . *deem* me less forgetful—is *per* diem. *By the day.* And like all per diem, it comes in the form of cash. Right? Am I makin' myself clear?

HOUSTON: You are trying to extort money from government officials. You are committing a—

ASHLEY: —Quiet, Mister, let him finish. Go ahead *(Deliberate)* . . . *George.*

HEWITT *(pause)*: Indeed. I am just taking care of business. We are not fooling one another here. We all know what's at stake for you and what's at stake for me. And we know they are different. I'm up there under oath—my ass is on the line. Now I've played with the big boys all my adult life—extortion? What brought me to Seattle, Mr. Prosecutor, a sick aunt?

ASHLEY: We get the picture. Agreed, gentlemen?

CANWELL: Any arrangement should have been made in New York before we brought him here. This is extremely distasteful. You work out the details with the general here.

ASHLEY: The committee have a discretionary funds account?

CANWELL: We can arrange a modest amount for living expenses—

HEWITT: —I haven't heard any figures being tossed around.

CANWELL: We are operating under a very austere budget here. I suppose we could come up with—

HEWITT: One hundred dollars a day.

HOUSTON: Are you crazy?

ASHLEY: One hundred dollars a day, cash, for every day you testify. That's what you're asking?

HEWITT: No. Not every day I testify. Every day I am away from my home. Today is day two.

HOUSTON: Ah . . .

ASHLEY: You are a son of a bitch, Hewitt. I don't like you at all.

HEWITT: Not many do, General. It comes with the territory. I'd like it at the end of each day. In twenties.

ASHLEY: I suggest you go along with providing per diem for . . . *Georgie* boy.

CANWELL: Very well. Mrs. Jaeger, here, will arrange it through my office.

HEWITT: And one further consideration. I was dragged out of downtown Manhattan yesterday, put on a plane—my wife is bound to be a bit—you gettin' the picture? We were a little short of cash when I left. Now, I want you to make this up to me. I want a hundred dollars sent by Western Union today. Miss, can you write this down? I want it sent to Mrs. Alethia Hewitt, 2750 Bronx Park Boulevard, number 4B. That's in the Bronx. Zone number 63. Is that clear?

ASHLEY: Agreed. The young lady will come with me, do you mind, dear? She'll wire a hundred dollars to your wife and then she'll bring another hundred to the hotel. We'll make arrangements for your reservation at the Roosevelt. If you do your job here like you're supposed to, you'll be back in New York with your family before you know it. (*Beat*) If you fuck with us while you're on the stand, you'll wish you never left the Soviet Union. Is that clear?

HEWITT: As a crystal ball.

ASHLEY: Now get down to work. Mrs. . . . . uh Jaeger? (*They start to leave.*)

HEWITT: One more detail. I'll be under oath. Perjury is a big load.

ASHLEY: No friendly witness has ever been or ever will be convicted of perjury. You have my word on that. Good day.

(ASHLEY *and* VIOLA *exit.* CANWELL *opens a file with photos and gives it to* HOUSTON.)

HOUSTON: We'd like you to identify these men, if any of them were at the school—the uh . . . farm?

HEWITT: Briehl's farm.

HOUSTON: Right. Will you be able to identify faces of anyone who was there?

HEWITT: Well, they all tend to look alike to me, but I'll do my best.

CANWELL: Ha, ha, ha. Sense of humor, Hewitt. I like that.

HOUSTON: You recognize him?

HEWITT: Not especially. Was he there?

HOUSTON: We have no idea. He certainly could have been.

HEWITT: What's his name?

CANWELL: Let's see. Gundlach. Professor. Psychology or philosophy, can't remember which.

HEWITT: Yeah. As long as he doesn't have some clear alibi, he could have been there.

HOUSTON: Can you be sure?

HEWITT: Don't you get it? If *you're* sure, *I'm* sure.

HOUSTON: I don't like this. We can't just accuse people of being where they weren't.

HEWITT: Wanna bet?

CANWELL: How about this joker?

HEWITT: He looks familiar.

CANWELL: He does? (HOUSTON *peers closer.*)

HEWITT: He looks like that movie actor . . . what's his name?

HOUSTON: An actor? You can't be sure then. You couldn't swear he was at the farm?

HEWITT: You still don't get it, do you? He might have been there and then again he might not have. I might have seen him in the papers—on a street corner or in the movies. My function here is not what you think it is. I just put my stamp of approval on what you guys come up with. You guys *accuse* the people and I say, "Yes suh, yes suh, yes suh." How many ways I gotta say it? How dense *are* you cats?

HOUSTON: Jesus Christ. Let's just send him back to New York. (*Beat*)

CANWELL: Not now, Bill, not now. (*He goes back to folder.*) Here's somebody. We happen to know that she made a trip to Soviet Russia in the thirties.

HEWITT: What year?

CANWELL: '34. When were you there?

HEWITT: From '29 to '32. I could probably stretch it.

CANWELL: The important fact is that she was in Russia. It's public record. The rest is details. She was there about the same time you were. We may have the year wrong.

HEWITT: Who is this woman?

CANWELL: Florence James. She and her old man run a theatre here. They teach a Russian acting technique. We wonder if she takes orders directly from the Kremlin.

HEWITT: Directly from the Kremlin? Oh, that's cute.

CANWELL: What?

HEWITT: Never mind. Go on.

CANWELL: So you didn't meet her over there?

HEWITT: No. I don't think so. But that doesn't mean anything. I didn't get hauled out to meet every American Communist who came to Moscow. Only when it served their own propaganda machine.

CANWELL: Then she could have been there, meeting with high-level Soviets, without you even knowing about it.

HEWITT: Well, hell yes.

HOUSTON: Do you have any qualms about identifying her?

HEWITT: Qualms? You keep asking me the wrong questions, Mister. (*To* CANWELL) How many are you going to want me to identify?

HOUSTON: No more than six or seven.

HEWITT: Six or seven? Haven't you got any—nobody is going to believe a hick burg like Seattle is producing half a dozen top-ranking, secret Party members.

CANWELL: Well, we want to be prudent, all right.

HEWITT: Prudent. You bet.

CANWELL: If we can nail Gundlach, Mrs. James in Russia, and uh . . . Rader. That would do fine. Just fine.

VIOLA (*entering*): Excuse me, Mr. Canwell?

CANWELL: Yes, what is it?

VIOLA: As we speak, the money is being wired to Mrs. Hewitt. And Mr. Hewitt has a room—with a view of Puget Sound . . . at the Roosevelt Hotel!

CANWELL: Thank you, Viol—Mrs. Jaeger.

VIOLA: You're welcome, sir.

CANWELL: One of my patrolmen will drive you there when we've finished. And I think we are.

VIOLA: I could drive him to the hotel.

CANWELL: Never mind. One of the State Police will escort him. You hear?

VIOLA: Yes, Mr. Canwell, it's just that you men are so busy.

CANWELL: You will do as I say. Right, Mr. Houston?

HOUSTON: What?

CANWELL: You'll get a State Patrolman to drive Mr. Hewitt to the hotel?

HOUSTON: I'll get a driver.

CANWELL (*aside to* HOUSTON): And by the way, don't wear cowboy boots at the hearing. Go buy some shoes. You're in the city now.

VIOLA: Did you hear that, Mr. Hewitt? You're staying at the Roosevelt Hotel!

[LIGHTS FADE]

SUPERTITLE:

THEATRE OF RECORD

The Hearings: A Public Accounting

July 1948

The hearing room as in act 1. The use of two witness stands may help expedite transitions between witnesses' testimonies.

CANWELL: Will you proceed, Mr. Houston, to call your first witness.

HOUSTON: Sophus Keith Winther. (WINTHER *is sworn in.*) Please state your name.

WINTHER: Sophus Keith Winther.

HOUSTON: And your occupation?

WINTHER: I am a professor at the University of Washington.

HOUSTON: What do you teach at the university?

WINTHER: English literature.

HOUSTON: Doctor, I will ask you if you have ever been a member of the Communist Party?

WINTHER: Yes, I was.

HOUSTON: Do you know about when you joined the Communist Party, Doctor?

WINTHER: I think it was in the spring of '35.

HOUSTON: And about how long did you remain a member of the Communist Party?

WINTHER: I know definitely the date when I withdrew from the Party, which was . . . that is, it was late November or December 1936.

HOUSTON: Of 1936. Speak loudly, Doctor, this is being recorded. Now do you know Professor Garland Ethel?

WINTHER (*glancing at each person before he responds*): Yes, I do.

HOUSTON: Was he a member of the Communist Party at the time

you were, Doctor?

WINTHER: Yes. That is, I assume he was and so that I can answer yes to your question, I was a member—at least I thought I was—I assumed that these others were.

HOUSTON: They attended meetings—

WINTHER: —Yes.

HOUSTON: Now, was Garland Ethel at such meetings?

WINTHER: Yes, he was.

HOUSTON: Was Professor Eby at these meetings, too?

WINTHER: Yes, he was.

CANWELL: Just a moment, Dr. Winther, will you respond a little louder. Your answer was "yes"?

WINTHER: Yes.

HOUSTON: Do you know Professor Eby's wife? Mrs. Lenna Eby?

WINTHER: Yes.

HOUSTON: And was she a member of the Communist Party?

WINTHER: Yes.

HOUSTON: Now, do you know Professor Herbert J. Phillips?

WINTHER: Yes, I do.

HOUSTON: Was Professor Phillips a member of the Communist Party?

WINTHER: Yes, on that same basis.

HOUSTON: On that same basis. Do you know Professor Phillips' wife?

WINTHER: Yes, I do.

HOUSTON: Was she in attendance at any of these meetings?

WINTHER: Yes, I think she was.

HOUSTON: Now, do you know Professor Angelo Pellegrini?

WINTHER: Yes, I do.

HOUSTON: Was Professor Pellegrini present at any of these meetings?

WINTHER: Yes, he was. I would like to make one qualifying remark since I recall him very well, and that is that he was a reluctant and uncooperative member of the unit.

HOUSTON: He wasn't a good Communist.

WINTHER: No. He was not.

HOUSTON: Was Mr. Pellegrini still a member when you left the Party?

WINTHER: I think he was but I could not be sure.

HOUSTON: Now, do you know Professor Melville Jacobs?

WINTHER: Yes.

HOUSTON: Was Professor Melville Jacobs a member of the Communist Party?

WINTHER: Yes.

HOUSTON: Now I will ask do you know Professor Joseph Butterworth?

WINTHER (*looks at* BUTTERWORTH, *pauses*): Yes, I do.

HOUSTON: Was he a member of the Communist Party at the time you were, Doctor?

WINTHER: Yes, he was.

HOUSTON: You paid dues in the Communist Party, didn't you? And you received a card in the Communist Party, didn't you?

WINTHER: I think I had some sort of an identification—I believe it was a book.

HOUSTON: A book. A little book with stamps in it.

PROJECTION:

A PHOTOCOPY OF A COMMUNIST PARTY STAMP BOOK

WINTHER: Yes.

HOUSTON: Now, do you know Professor Melvin Rader?

WINTHER: Yes, I do.

HOUSTON: Mr. Chairman, I believe that is all from this witness.

CANWELL: You don't intend to leave town in the next week or so, do you?

WINTHER: No.

CANWELL: On the understanding, Dr. Winther, that you will be on call if the committee wishes to hear from you again, I will release you from the subpoena and wish to thank you sincerely for your appearance here.

HOUSTON: You can deposit that subpoena with Mr. Robinson over there and receive your witness—and receive your witness fee— (*Pointedly*)—two dollars, (*Beat*) which the State allows witnesses.

(WINTHER *leaves the stand, awkwardly making his way to the table and receiving his witness fee.* HERBERT J. PHILLIPS, *having arrived from New York, enters through the audience, looks around, sees* JOHN CAUGHLAN, *goes to him, and sits beside him.* PHOTOGRAPHERS *take pictures.*)

HOUSTON: Will Mr. Angelo Pellegrini come forward?

(*Cameras flash.* PELLEGRINI *is paraded for the press as he is sworn in.*)

HOUSTON: Will you please state your name?

PELLEGRINI: Angelo Pellegrini.

HOUSTON: What is your occupation, Mr. Pellegrini?

PELLEGRINI: I am a teacher at the university in the English Department.

HOUSTON: Where were you born, Mr. Pellegrini?

PELLEGRINI: In Italy.

HOUSTON: When did you come to this country?

PELLEGRINI: In 1913.

HOUSTON: In 1913. I will ask you, Mr. Pellegrini, are you or have you ever been a member of the Communist Party?

PELLEGRINI: I was a member of the Communist Party sometime in the middle thirties.

(*Cameras flash.*)

HOUSTON: Do you recall the year you joined?

PELLEGRINI: I don't recall it exactly but it's somewhere in '35 and '36.

HOUSTON: About how long were you a member of the Communist Party?

PELLEGRINI: I should say somewhere within a year.

HOUSTON: Within a year. You don't recall?

PELLEGRINI: I don't recall—I don't recall exactly.

HOUSTON: Now, you know the names of practically all the professors that were mentioned here earlier, do you not? You know these professors?

PELLEGRINI: Yes, I do.

HOUSTON: Did you meet with any of these men in the Communist Party meetings?

PELLEGRINI: I can't remember having met in a closed meeting with any one of these individuals that was named.

HOUSTON: Was Harold Eby present at any of these meetings that you attended?

PELLEGRINI (*pause*): Not that I can recollect.

HOUSTON: Not that you recollect. Would you remember if a faculty member was present at these meetings?

PELLEGRINI: I'm not sure that I would. There were many meetings, open meetings, closed meetings. There were long communist meetings and the whole thing is just a vague blur in my mind.

HOUSTON: Do you mean to tell me that you cannot name a single man that you sat in Communist Party meetings with?

PELLEGRINI: I . . . I don't recollect any of that I can say for sure.

HOUSTON: If you could recall some of these people that you met with, you would testify to that fact from this witness stand?

PELLEGRINI: Well, I think that's a hypothetical question. It really isn't involved, is it?

HOUSTON: If you could recall any details, would you testify to them here, today?

PELLEGRINI: I think I would.

HOUSTON: Do you want to make that stronger than say, "I think I would"? Is there any doubt in your mind?

PELLEGRINI (*pause*): No, there isn't.

HOUSTON: Well, if there is no doubt then, would you testify to them or would you not?

PELLEGRINI: I would, sir.

HOUSTON: You would. Mr. Chairman, I suggest that this committee—that this man not be excused from the subpoena—that he be asked to step aside from the witness stand now and it may be possible that the crowd and the group of people here that—has this loss of memory, maybe before this hearing is over be able to recall some—to the details of these meetings.

CANWELL: The witness is directed to step aside and remain in attendance for future call to the witness stand. You may step aside now, Mr. Pellegrini. Please call your next witness.

HOUSTON: Will Mr. Garland Ethel please step forward.

(ETHEL *is sworn in.*)

HOUSTON: Will you please state your name?

ETHEL: Garland Ethel.

HOUSTON: Fine. What is your occupation?

ETHEL: I'm a teacher of English literature at the University of Washington.

HOUSTON: Doctor, I will ask you, are you or have you ever been a member of the Communist Party?

ETHEL: I am not a member of the Communist Party, but I have been a member of the Communist Party. So far as my behavior is concerned, I consider that adult and responsible. I take full consequences for everything I've done anytime in my life, and so far as my behavior is concerned, I am completely willing to talk unreservedly about myself. Anything you ask me about me, I will answer with complete disclosure. Now, I should like to continue with a statement relative to other persons. I told you that I was unwilling to name other persons as Communists or possible Communists for two reasons. One is that I didn't have knowledge about their membership. The other point was that my own particular code of honor forbids that kind of naming of persons to their possible injury, but most of all it's a question of living up to my own standard of conduct. Now, that happens to be my situation; I have a standard of honor, and that standard is not to name other persons, and I told you that would be my position. That is my position, sir.

HOUSTON (*pause*): Dr. Ethel, have you ever attended any Communist Party meetings with Harold Eby?

ETHEL (*pause*): I shall have to decline, sir, on the general rule that I have just announced, that that is not compatible with my code, and if I have your permission, I'll add a word or so—

HOUSTON: —You'll what?

ETHEL: Add a word or two of explanation—

HOUSTON: —No, I want your answer to be responsive.

ETHEL (*pause*): Yes, sir.

HOUSTON: Have you ever attended any Communist Party meetings with Ralph Gundlach?

ETHEL: I am going to decline again on the same grounds, sir. It's naming the person. I said I was unwilling to do that—

HOUSTON: —Have you ever attended any Communist Party meetings with Joseph Butterworth?

ETHEL: Again, I repeat exactly the same position, sir—

HOUSTON: —Have you ever attended any Communist Party meetings with Herbert J. Phillips?

ETHEL: Once more, sir, now I'm sorry to take up the time, but I must decline to answer that on the same grounds.

HOUSTON: Mr. Chairman, it is very clear that the witness refuses to answer proper and pertinent questions.

CANWELL: Let me state that we are specifically interested in obtaining information which we feel we are authorized to elicit; and I will repeat the questions asked by Mr. Houston as to whether you have attended closed Party meetings with Professor Butterworth or Professor Phillips or Professor Grundlach.

ETHEL: Yes, I understand.

CANWELL: Do you refuse to answer?

ETHEL: Yes, sir. I decline to answer those questions.

HOUSTON: Mr. Chairman, I ask that this witness be excused.

CANWELL: No, we will not excuse the witness; we will ask the witness to step aside and remain in attendance until the committee decides what action to take on your refusal to give this testimony in this hearing. You may step aside.

ETHEL: Well, may I ask one question of you, sir, a question of permission?

CANWELL (*gavels*): No, you may—we will not permit this to go on. Either you will answer the questions, the proper questions of this committee or the questions we believe to be proper, or you will step aside until we wish to call you to the stand again.

ETHEL: Yes, sir.

CANWELL: I will ask you to step aside and remain in attendance until formally released from the subpoena.

(*Applause and a demonstration commences.*)

CANWELL (*gaveling*): If there are any further demonstrations by the audience, we will ask the State Patrol to remove those participating in said demonstrations, and upon removal said demonstrators will remain out of the hearing room during the course of these hearings.

CAUGHLAN (*coming forward with document*): May I hand you—

CANWELL: You may leave it at the office if you wish or take it up with us at the close of the hearing. (*To a* STAFF MEMBER) You may take this communication, someone from the staff—

(MRS. JAMES *is passing out copies of a statement to audience, the press, and witnesses.* CANWELL *notices.*)

CANWELL (*gavels, then shouting to* MRS. JAMES): You will desist in passing out literature or press reports or whatever they may be at this hearing! You'll have to do it outside this hearing. I wish to again caution against any demonstrations by the audience. (CAUGHLAN *is roughly escorted back to his seat by a* STATE PA-TROLMAN. MRS. JAMES *continues to pass out flyers.*) I feel that having been cautioned, if there are demonstrations, we will be justified in requesting arrests; because of—of information supplied this committee, I want to state it so that no one will misunderstand, that we will not tolerate any interference with the orderly procedure of this hearing.

MRS. JAMES: Mr. Chairman, may I present an important communication from me and my associates?

CANWELL: You may do so in writing.

MRS. JAMES: May I explain for the record what the subjects of this communication are?

CANWELL (*gavels*): No. There will not be speeches in this hearing from the back of the room. We will not attempt to proceed until we have order.

(MRS. JAMES *is forcibly removed from the hearing room by several* STATE PATROLMEN. *She is lifted up and handed hand over hand, horizontally, to the aisle. People in the audience stand up to see the eviction.* PHOTOGRAPHERS *leave their seats to get closer and take pictures. Flash bulbs pop. Shouting.* CANWELL *gavels.* PATROLMEN *restore order.*)

HOUSTON: Mr. Chairman, due to the demonstration we have just had, I wish to call this witness temporarily out of order for just a few questions, out of order.

CANWELL: You may proceed.

(HEWITT *is sworn in.*)

HOUSTON: Will you please state your name?

HEWITT: George Hewitt.

HOUSTON: Of what city are you a resident, Mr. Hewitt?

HEWITT: New York City.

HOUSTON: I will ask you, Mr. Hewitt, are you or have you ever been a member of the Communist Party?

HEWITT: Yes, sir, for eighteen years.

HOUSTON: Have you ever visited Russia?

HEWITT: Yes, sir. I visited Russia from 1930 to 1934.

HOUSTON: 1930 to 1934, and you worked and taught in Russia, is that right?

HEWITT: I did, yes, sir.

HOUSTON: I will ask you, Mr. Hewitt, if you observed the demonstration that we just had here.

HEWITT: I did.

HOUSTON: Do you recognize the lady that made that demonstration?

HEWITT: Yes, sir, I do.

HOUSTON: Do you know what the lady's name is?

HEWITT (*pause*): Mrs. James.

HOUSTON: Mrs. James. Where did you first meet Mrs. James?

HEWITT: I met Mrs. James, first, in the Profintern Building in Russia, Moscow.

HOUSTON: You met Mrs. James in the Profintern Building in Moscow, Russia?

HEWITT: First. Secondly, at the Comintern Headquarters, which is known as the Communist International Headquarters.

HOUSTON: Is that also in the city of Moscow?

HEWITT: In the city of Moscow.

HOUSTON: In Russia?

HEWITT: And then, thirdly, at a visit of the Lenin School.

HOUSTON: At a visit of the Lenin School. Did she inform you, and did you find out from her that she was from the United States?

HEWITT: Yes, sir. We were told that she was one of the "sparks" to be used to develop on the cultural field agitation for the Soviet government, in the United States.

HOUSTON: Agitation for the Soviet government, on the cultural field, in the United States. Uh-huh. Did she admit to you, or did information come into your hands, that she was a member of the American Communist Party?

HEWITT: Yes, sir.

HOUSTON: Mr. Chairman, I ask that this witness step aside. We intend to use him for some other issues, later. It was just this phase I wanted to put on now.

(HEWITT *leaves the stand.*)

CANWELL: I wish to state that the witnesses under subpoena, who were caused to be removed from the room, are not excused from attendance at this hearing and must remain on call. Their expulsion from the hearing room does not excuse them from their subpoena.

HOUSTON: I suggest we call Professor Phillips, who I see is here with his counsel, is that correct?

(PHILLIPS *and* CAUGHLAN *go to witness chairs.* CAUGHLAN *remains standing.*)

CANWELL: Will you be seated, Mr. Caughlan?

CAUGHLAN: Mr. Chairman, may I—

CANWELL (*gavels*): Mr. Caughlan, will you be seated, and we—

CAUGHLAN: May I be—

(*A* STATE PATROLMAN *standing behind* CAUGHLAN *forces him back in the chair.*)

CANWELL: —we will tell you what you can do—

CAUGHLAN: —advised of the procedure because I want to know—

CANWELL: —The procedure followed here will be that you may freely counsel with your attorney, quietly. There will be no speeches made in this hearing room by counsel for any witness. We merely want the answers to certain questions which this committee feels we are authorized to ask.

CAUGHLAN: I have a question to ask—

CANWELL (*gavels*): —You will ask no more questions! We are not going to go on with any ridiculous procedure here. You will either comply with the instructions of the committee or you will be removed. Now, let's understand that for good. You are going to comply with the procedure here, or you are not going to be here.

(STATE PATROLMAN *pushes* CAUGHLAN *down in his chair.*)

CAUGHLAN: I haven't even had a chance to talk with him.

CANWELL: You may advise him as . . . whether or not to answer, and that is all you may advise him in this hearing. Now, with that understanding, we will proceed; otherwise, you will be removed. (*Pause*) Well, I think we will proceed.

HOUSTON: Will you please state your name?

PHILLIPS: Herbert J. Phillips.

HOUSTON: What is your occupation, Mr. Phillips?

PHILLIPS: Teacher at the university.

HOUSTON: What university?

PHILLIPS: University of Washington.

HOUSTON: Mr. Phillips, I will ask you if you are or have you ever been a member of the Communist Party?

PHILLIPS: For conscience . . . conscience sake, and political sake, I refuse to answer the question.

CANWELL: Put the question to Mr. Phillips again. I wish to advise you too, Mr. Phillips, that your failure to respond to answer this question will be considered a refusal to testify and will be the termination of your testimony before this committee.

CAUGHLAN: May I state—

CANWELL (*gavels*): No, you may . . . you may speak to your client quietly, but you may state nothing for the hearing.

HOUSTON: Mr. Phillips, I will ask you if you are or have you ever been a member of the Communist Party?

PHILLIPS: I must say that in light of the testimony that has previously been given that I would regard it a violation of my principles, a violation of what I regard to be the most sacred—

HOUSTON: Mr. Chairman, he is attempting to make a speech and not be responsive, and that he be instructed to answer the question "yes" or "no."

CANWELL: Now, *I* will ask you, Mr. Phillips, if you have, if you are now, or have ever been, a member of the Communist Party.

PHILLIPS: I will not answer that question.

CANWELL: Step aside.

CAUGHLAN (*standing up*): May I—

CANWELL: You aren't saying anything in here, and you may proceed directly from the hearing room. Now, we do not care to go into this question of the witness's contempt under your instructions. Now, if you will remove yourself from the room, you will save us the trouble. (CAUGHLAN *stands defiantly.*) You have no client on the stand now. (*Pause*) We will hold you in contempt in a moment, if you continue your obstinate attitude. (CAUGHLAN *sits.*) I wish to make a statement for the record, regarding one John Caughlan.

CAUGHLAN (*quickly standing up again*): Yes, sir.

CANWELL (*gavels*): You will be seated, Mr. Caughlan. (CAUGHLAN *is forced to sit.*) Mr. Caughlan has been permitted to appear here as counsel for some of the principals named in this hearing. He has been advised specifically what his standing is in that regard. Personally, Mr. Caughlan was mentioned many times as a Communist Party member. If he persists in trying to disrupt these hearings, he will be removed, regardless of his — the wish of his clients to represent them. Personally, before this committee, he has no standing as an attorney, or as a citizen, or as a man. We have a very poor regard of Mr. Caughlan, but we are permitting him to represent his client here, but only on the terms which we specify. Now, if Mr. Caughlan wishes to conform to those terms, he may remain here. Otherwise, he will have to be removed and will have to stay out of here. Now that is the opinion of this committee, and we will have no more foolishness about it.

ATTORNEY O'BRIEN (*from the audience*): May I ask a question as counsel for a witness? I want to inquire, Mr. Chairman, whether the committee is presuming to instruct counsel in their duty to their clients?

CANWELL: We are not even going to discuss the thing further here and we will tolerate no more interference from counsel from the back of the room and I am instructing the State Patrol at this moment that if we have any more such demonstrations, or attempts of counsel to inject their opinions or ideas or whatever they have in mind into this hearing from the back of the room that they will be removed and kept out of this hearing. Now if that is not plain enough, why, we will have to depend on the State Patrol to take it from there.

O'BRIEN: I bow to force.

(*There is a demonstration in audience.*)

CANWELL: Will the State Patrol take those youngsters back there who are demonstrating out of the room, and the instructions of this committee is if anyone who demonstrates in similar circumstances again, will be removed and will stay out of the hearing room. Now we are not going to tolerate much more foolishness. The boy with the yellow sweater, take him out!

(*The demonstration subsides but it is still tense in the room.*)

HOUSTON: Will Joseph Butterworth take the stand, please?

HATTEN: Mr. Chairman, I am C. T. Hatten, attorney for Mr. Butterworth.

(BUTTERWORTH *and* HATTEN *come to the witness table.*)

CANWELL: Before we proceed, I want to be sure that counsel for Mr. Butterworth understands that his position here as counsel for his client is limited to the right to confer with his client and not to make speeches, and now we will proceed and Mr. Butterworth will be sworn.

HATTEN: Mr. Canwell—

CANWELL: —Stand and be sworn—

HATTEN: —I insist on—

CANWELL: —You will be seated or you will be removed. (*A* STATE PATROLMAN *forces* HATTEN *down into chair.*) Now just retain your proper position—

HATTEN: —legal objections.

BUTTERWORTH: Under duress I will be sworn.

CANWELL: We are not interested in your qualifications, but do you solemnly swear that the testimony you are about to give here will be the truth, the whole truth, and nothing but the truth, so help you God?

(BUTTERWORTH *sits.*)

HOUSTON: Will you please state your name?

BUTTERWORTH: My name is Joseph Butterworth.

HOUSTON: What is your occupation, Mr. Butterworth?

BUTTERWORTH: I teach on the university campus—University of Washington.

HOUSTON: What do you teach?

BUTTERWORTH: I teach English.

HOUSTON: How long have you been employed by the University of Washington?

BUTTERWORTH: Nineteen years.

HOUSTON: Mr. Butterworth, are you or have you ever been a member of the Communist Party?

HATTEN: I object to that question, Your Honor.

CANWELL: You will make no further vocal objections, Mr. Hatten. If you do, you will be removed. Now, Mr. Butterworth may answer the question.

HATTEN: I advise you not to answer the question.

BUTTERWORTH: Mr. Chairman, because of conscience and because I should not have to testify against myself, I will decline to answer that question.

HATTEN: The right of cross-examination—

CANWELL (*gavels*): Will you remove Mr. Hatten from the room?

(HATTEN *is ejected from the hearing by a* STATE PATROLMAN.)

CAUGHLAN: Mr. Chairman, there is nothing on the record to show—

CANWELL: Mr. Caughlan is not to return to this hearing room again while this hearing is in session. If he does, I am instructing the State Patrol to put—place him under arrest.

(CAUGHLAN *is also ejected from the hearing by a* STATE PATROL-MAN.)

BUTTERWORTH: Mr. Chairman, I am not represented by counsel.

CANWELL: Will you ask the question again, Mr. Houston?

HOUSTON: Mr. Butterworth, are you or have you ever been a member of the Communist Party?

BUTTERWORTH: Because of conscience, and because I—this body has no right to force me to testify against myself. I refuse to answer the question.

CANWELL: You refuse to answer the question?

BUTTERWORTH: I do.

CANWELL: You may step aside, Mr. Butterworth. (BUTTERWORTH *leaves the stand.*)

(*At this point, lighting, sound, and staging should suggest a montage of the following testimony.*)

(*Lights come up on* MELVILLE JACOBS *in midtestimony.*)

JACOBS: . . . I am very sorry, Mr. Houston, but I cannot, I simply cannot, be an informer on people who, in my judgment, have always been completely loyal to our country, and who do not believe in force and violence, who have never done anything illegal and who are my friends.

CANWELL: The committee will proceed against you to have you cited for contempt of the legislature for refusing to answer the questions of the committee.

JACOBS: I cannot answer, Mr. Canwell.

CANWELL: You may step aside.

JACOBS: Thank you. (JACOBS *leaves witness stand.*)

(*Lights fade and come up on* RALPH GUNDLACH *in midtestimony.*)

HOUSTON: I will ask you if you are, or ever have been, a member of the Communist Party.

GUNDLACH: Mr. Houston, no one has the right to ask about one's personal beliefs or associations. It's like asking, "When did you stop beating your wife?"

CANWELL: Now I will ask you, are you or have you ever been a member of the Communist Party?

GUNDLACH: I think the question implies subversive activities. I am willing to testify to any legitimate question.

CANWELL: We will determine whether or not that is legitimate. If you refuse to answer, you may step aside. You are not excused.

HOUSTON: Will Mr. George Hewitt take the stand again? (HEWITT *does so.*) Will you please state your name?

HEWITT: George Hewitt.

HOUSTON: Mr. Hewitt, are you now, or have you ever been, a member of the Communist Party?

HEWITT: Yes, sir, I have been a member of the Communist Party since 1926. I left in 1944.

HOUSTON: Have you ever held office or positions in the Communist Party?

HEWITT: Yes, sir.

HOUSTON: Now, does the Communist Party attempt especially to recruit Negro people into its ranks?

HEWITT: Yes, sir. They have had for a number of years all types of methods to attract the Negro people.

HOUSTON: You went to Russia under the auspices and instructions of the Communist Party, did you not?

HEWITT: I did.

HOUSTON: And when was this?

HEWITT: That was the latter part of 1929.

HOUSTON: You went to Russia, then, in the latter part of 1929. You remained in Russia until approximately 1934.

HEWITT: About . . . I would say 1933.

(HOUSTON *and* CANWELL *shoot each other glances.*)

HOUSTON: '33.

HEWITT: Yes, sir.

HOUSTON: Now, Mr. Hewitt, were you ever in the city of Seattle before in your life until you came to this hearing?

HEWITT: This is the first time.

HOUSTON: Since you have been in attendance in this room, have you seen any people that you've recognized?

HEWITT: Yes, sir.

HOUSTON: Would you name those people that you recognize?

HEWITT: Well, Professor Gundlach.

HOUSTON: Professor Gundlach, Professor Ralph H. Gundlach?

HEWITT: That's right.

HOUSTON: Anybody else?

HEWITT: Mrs. James.

HOUSTON: Mrs. Florence Bean James?

HEWITT: That's right.

HOUSTON: Anybody else?

HEWITT: Professor Rader.

HOUSTON: Professor Rader. Is that Professor Melvin Rader?

HEWITT: Melvin Rader.

HOUSTON (*pointing to* RADER): He is the man that—you're positive of your identification?

HEWITT: Very definite.

HOUSTON: All right. Now, let's go back, and suppose you tell us the circumstances under which you met Professor Ralph H. Gundlach.

HEWITT: In the state of New York, in the year of 1938 and '39, there was, for the first time, a practical attempt made to carry out the decisions of the conference that we had in Moscow. It was the first secret school of professionals ever held in this country. It had about seventy students. I taught in this school, where I had occasion to meet and converse with a number of these communist professors, under strict obligations of secrecy.

HOUSTON: Now, where was this school held?

HEWITT: Up near Kingston, New York, on Briehl's farm, B-r-i-e-h-l.

HOUSTON: And that's the one that had the seventy students.

HEWITT: That's right.

HOUSTON: Now, these students, you say, were professional men. Were they prominently teachers or engineers or lawyers or what?

HEWITT: Teachers from universities.

HOUSTON: Teachers from universities. Now, how were these people selected, to be in attendance there?

HEWITT: Very carefully, by the National Board or National Committee of the Party.

HOUSTON: Were they selected from all over the United States?

HEWITT: Yes, sir.

HOUSTON: Now, I will ask you if any of the men you have named were in attendance?

HEWITT: Professor Gundlach.

HOUSTON: And he attended this secret communist school. Is there a shadow of a doubt as to whether he could have attended that school and not have been a member of the Communist Party?

HEWITT: No, sir, he could not. He would have to be a member of the Communist Party to attend that school.

HOUSTON: Did Professor Melvin Rader attend that school?

HEWITT (*a pause, then*): The same answer applies.

HOUSTON: Now you are positive that that is the Melvin Rader you have seen here in this room?

HEWITT: Yes, sir.

HOUSTON: Now what year was this school held?

HEWITT: That was in the . . . about the year '39 . . . '38 and '39.

HOUSTON: '38 and '39. How long was the course?

HEWITT: It was supposed to be a course of a month and a half.

HOUSTON: Six weeks. This was secret, completely from the public.

HEWITT: Definitely.

HOUSTON: Was this school . . . did it teach revolution against the government of the United States?

HEWITT: Yes, sir. It taught Marxism, Leninism, political economy, you teach the dictatorship of the proletariat, which means how to overthrow the capitalist form of government.

HOUSTON: Now, I will ask you, Mr. Hewitt, just so we won't leave it hanging in the air, your recognition of Mrs. James was not in connection with this school?

HEWITT: No, sir.

HOUSTON: Now, just before—I don't—we've got to hurry along— but in your earlier testimony you stated that you had seen a woman by the name of Florence Bean James in Russia?

HEWITT: Yes, sir, one of the most popular places for people of the cultural field—center, I would say—in Moscow was known as the Meyerhold Theatre. I was very intimate with the aides of Mr. Meyerhold.

HOUSTON: How do you spell that?

HEWITT: M-e-y-e-r-h-o-l-d. It was the Repertory Theatre of Moscow. I was very intimate with these people and discussed, very loosely, the Americans who would come to Mrs. James.

BURTON JAMES (*standing and shouting*): You're a liar!

CANWELL: We will proceed with no further disturbances from the back of the room.

JAMES (*from the back of the room*): Mr. Chairman, this committee—

CANWELL: —I will ask to have you removed, Mr. James, if we have any further outburst back there.

JAMES (*shouting*): Perjurer! She went to Russia in '34!

CANWELL: Take him out. (JAMES *is forcibly removed.*) I wish to state, also, that we cannot, as a committee of the legislature, permit the Communists, their friends, or advisors to take over a function of the legislature. Shall we proceed?

HOUSTON: Yes, sir. You saw this party, Mrs. James, in Moscow, when?

HEWITT: 1932. (*Pause while* HOUSTON, *caught off guard, looks at him.*) To be given decisions on the forthcoming Paris convention of culture that was eventually held in 1934.

HOUSTON (*trying to compose himself*): You saw this person over a period of several weeks?

HEWITT: About two to three weeks. It's quite possible that in the sequence of dates that one could confuse a certain date, such as dates eighteen years back. I'm not an authority on remembering time, hours, days, but generally one can fit a certain situation in a category of events. It's very definite that the people were there in 1932, without question of a doubt.

HOUSTON: Now you testified that two people were there . . . at Briehl's farm.

HEWITT: Yes, sir.

HOUSTON: Now, you are positive of this?

HEWITT: Definitely.

HOUSTON: No question of doubt?

HEWITT: No, sir.

(*Lights fade and come up on* MRS. JAMES, *testifying.*)

HOUSTON: Will you please state your name?

MRS. JAMES: Florence Bean James.

HOUSTON: What is your occupation, Mrs. James?

MRS. JAMES: I am codirector of the Repertory—Seattle Repertory Playhouse.

HOUSTON: Mrs. James, I will ask you if you are, or ever have been, a member of the Communist Party.

MRS. JAMES: Mr. Houston, I resist with everything I have your right to ask that question, and I stand on my constitutional rights to refuse to answer it.

CANWELL: We wish to advise you so there will be no mistake. You may answer "yes" or "no," or we will cite you for contempt.

HOUSTON: Mrs. James, are you or have you ever been a member of the Communist Party?

MRS. JAMES: Mr. Houston, I feel that I have answered the question.

CANWELL: You refuse to answer the question, then?

MRS. JAMES: I have answered it.

CANWELL: You refuse to answer it with a "yes" or "no" answer?

MRS. JAMES: I have answered.

CANWELL: Step aside.

(Lights fade and come up on BURTON JAMES, *testifying.)*

HOUSTON: Will you please state your name?

BURTON: Burton W. James.

HOUSTON: What is your business, Mr. James?

BURTON: I'm the codirector of the Seattle Repertory Playhouse.

HOUSTON: Mr. James—

BURTON: —I do not care to answer further.

HOUSTON: Mr. James, are you or have you ever been a member of the Communist Party?

BURTON: I do not care to answer.

CANWELL: Then step aside, please.

(*A* STATE PATROLMAN *enters and gives* CANWELL *a piece of paper, which he reads.*)

CANWELL: I would like to call a 15-minute recess at this time. (CANWELL *gavels, rises, and exits.*)

[LIGHTS FADE]

SUPERTITLE:

THEATRE OF CONJECTURE

The Recess

CANWELL, HEWITT, *and* HOUSTON *move downstage left, and* NIENDORFF *enters from another direction.*

NIENDORFF: What gives? Everyone looks—

CANWELL: —Mr. Hewitt is tired.

HEWITT: I am not tired—

CANWELL: —Mr. Hewitt is not well—he needs a rest. He can't— the King County prosecutor was here. He talked to Senator Kimball and myself out in the hallway. Gundlach has filed some charges. He said Rader is about to file too. He wants to cross-examine Mr. Hewitt on his testimony thus far. Even before we get Rader on the stand—here in our offices.

NIENDORFF: Well, he's immune, for Chrissake, isn't he? The com-mittee has legislative immunity from cross-examination, that's what we've been—

HOUSTON: —Only from witnesses' attorneys. If there is a question of a law being broken during the hearing—say, for instance, perjury—they can ask, as a courtesy, to cross-examine, in a private setting, since it may be a matter of interest to the City to prosecute. Was there any paper?

CANWELL: Just a note requesting the cross-examination.

HOUSTON: Let's see it.

CANWELL: I tore it up.

HOUSTON: You did what?

CANWELL: I tore it up in his face.

HOUSTON: Not smart—

CANWELL: —They can't do this. I won't let them—is the prosecutor a Red too? What's his name? I won't allow this to happen, do you hear? I'll surround the armory with the State Patrol—the National Guard if I need to. I didn't bring these hearings to life in order to have some communist turncoat . . . destroy them with reckless talk—loose talk—unsubstantiated—I knew he wouldn't be smart enough to pull this off—

HEWITT: Oh, Mr. Canwell. Mr. Canwell. I don't think my intelligence is the issue here. I just did what I was told, like I said I would. If you can't handle explosives, what are you doing lighting matches?

HOUSTON: If we can just stave off the city prosecutor until we get Rader on the stand—I can break him. I know I can. He's bound to contradict himself. I can bully him into submission—

NIENDORFF: George here doesn't need to be here for that. Isn't he done? You done? You got more to say? He have more to say?

HOUSTON: I need him in the room during Rader's testimony. I want him to help me rattle him. I want him to stare Rader down. I want him to scoff at his testimony. I want him to put on his *own* little demonstration just like they have been doing to us. Everyone in the room will be watching his reaction to Rader's story. He's essential. I need him to—

NIENDORFF: I think not. I don't think he should be available—

CANWELL: —That's what I'm telling you. George Hewitt is not feeling well. He's exhausted from—

NIENDORFF: Get him out of town.

HOUSTON: What? No—

NIENDORFF: We gotta get him out of here fast.

CANWELL: Is there a flight out of here this afternoon?

HEWITT: Who are you talking about? Is it me? Have I disappeared? I am *here!* You want something out of me, you talk to *me!* (*Pause*) Must you *people*—talk about me in my presence like I wasn't *here?* I am not a piece of tissue you've blown your noses in and dropped on the floor. It is all so amazing, so . . . never mind. I *am* tired. You people with your little bit of almighty *position*—you just . . . make me bone weary.

CANWELL: I don't think you are in any shape to continue here. I think you are emotionally—

HEWITT: —Put me on a plane, will you? Can you do that for me? I want to go back to . . . Can you get me on a plane . . . and I'll be on my way.

NIENDORFF: Airlines don't fly East this time of day. There will be one tonight around ten.

CANWELL: That's too late. Put him on a train. Just get him out of town this afternoon and then— We'll get one of the State Patrol to drive him to Union Station.

HOUSTON: No. I don't think we want any official help in Mr. Hewitt's departure from Seattle. Lots of people are going to ask a lot of questions about Mr. Hewitt's whereabouts.

NIENDORFF: Viola.

HOUSTON: Who?

NIENDORFF: Viola. I'll call her.

CANWELL: I don't think that's . . . couldn't *you* . . . ?

NIENDORFF: It so happens I am covering these hearings for my paper. I have to see them in order to write about them. Would those arrangements suit you, Mr. Hewitt? I'll have Viola drive you to the station as soon as she can get here. If anyone asks, tell 'em he went . . . to the *airport.* He was finished testifying and had to get back to his family. His wife is expecting a baby. I'll call Viola. We gotta get outta here. Why don't you come across the street with me, Mr. Hewitt, and I'll buy you a refreshment, while we wait for Viola. Don't resume the hearings till I get back. Mr. Hewitt, I certainly thank you for your citizenship while here in Seattle. How about you boys?

CANWELL: Uh . . . of course . . . Mr. Hewitt. It was a pleasure . . . uh . . . I mean, I want to thank you on behalf of the committee . . . uh . . . I know this must have been—you have a pleasant trip—

HEWITT: —Mr. Canwell. Don't bother, don't even try. (*Pause*) You know something? You guys are amateurs. You're laughable. In *Stalin's* purge trials they did their homework. They broke the witnesses way before they got them on the stand. They were smart enough to know you can't leave anything to chance. You guys should still be in the back rooms breaking skulls and threatening their children. You're showing the public a bad rehearsal—

CANWELL: Get out of here! We are civilized people here. We have the rule of law—

HEWITT: —Right. I wouldn't trade places with any of you. Not for anything. I *know* what I am. And I know what I do. I destroy people and I do it at the behest of *other* people. It's not a pretty sight, is it? But I'll tell you what. You *like* it. You do it of your own . . . *volition.* I *know* when I'm eating shit. That's the difference. You *pretend* you're eating wafers and drinking wine.

CANWELL (*pause*): It's unusual to meet a Negro Catholic.

NIENDORFF (*slight pause*): Let's go, Mr. Hewitt.

(NIENDORFF *and* HEWITT *exit.*)

CANWELL: Good. That's settled. (*To* HOUSTON) Now. I want you to make mincemeat out of Melvin Rader.

[LIGHTS FADE]

[END OF ACT TWO]

Act 3, "Melvin Rader Takes the Stand": Michael Lopez (Eby), Jason Gingold (Rader), Pace Ebbesen (Astley).

ACT THREE

SUPERTITLE:

THEATRE OF RECORD

Melvin Rader Takes the Stand

July 1948

The hearings resume as RADER *takes the stand with his attorney,*
ED HENRY.

HOUSTON: What is your name?

RADER: Melvin Rader.

HOUSTON: Where do you live, Mr. Rader?

RADER: In the city of Seattle.

HOUSTON: And how long have you lived in the city of Seattle?

RADER: I have been here since 1921. I came here as a student the
first time—

HOUSTON: —Mr. Rader, I will ask you, are you or have you ever
been a member of the Communist Party?

RADER: I will answer the question "no." I have never been a member of the Communist Party, and I am not now a member of
the Communist Party.

HOUSTON: Now, I will ask you, Professor, if you were ever a member of an organization known as the League Against War and
Fascism, which has been declared a subversive organization by

the attorney general of the United States of America?

RADER: I have been a member of the American League Against War and Fascism.

HOUSTON: From 1936, did you believe in the collective security in the grouping of the democracies of the world against the fascist countries?

RADER: Well, sir, in 1936 . . . you say in 1936?

HOUSTON: Yes.

RADER: Until—until—

HOUSTON: Yes, until we had the switch in the—turn in the railroads. I will be explicit if you want me to, on the date.

RADER: Now, wait a minute. I'm not limiting this to any period that can be characterized in terms of a switch. Now in 1936, and continuously, I think, right up to the present time, I have believed in the principle of what we have now come to call the United Nations.

HOUSTON: Are you conversant that in 1936 there was a switch in the Communist Party line after the speech by Mr. Dimitrov on the orientation and the starting of the United Front program?

RADER: In 1936. About what—what time in 1936?

CANWELL: I think we might dispense with these dialectical discussions and—

(Laughter and applause from some of the audience—gaveling.)

HOUSTON: Mr. Chairman, I . . . the man has no memory, and I am giving him specific dates and places; and if he wants to—

CANWELL: Well, have you followed the Communist Party line, Doctor?

RADER: I have never been and I am not now a follower of the Communist Party line. I have reached all my decisions independently, as an individual, and never at the behest or the instruction or the dictation of the Communist Party or any communist front organization or any other party or organization.

HOUSTON: Now, were you one of the sponsors of the Harry Bridges Defense Committee? Were you on that committee?

RADER: Well, sir, I may be mistaken. I don't remember whether I was on that committee or not. If there is any clear evidence I was that seems convincing to me, I will certainly be glad to say "yes."

HOUSTON: May I refresh your memory. June 30th of 1939 of the *Post-Intelligencer,* a Seattle newspaper, under the heading, "Bridges Defense Committee Formed. Listed as a member of the Committee are Professors Harold Eby, Garland Ethel, and Melvin Rader."

RADER: Well, sir, I don't regard the *Post-Intelligencer* as always accurate. I am willing to say that there is some presumptive evidence here.

HOUSTON: Well, now, you heard the testimony earlier of the witness George Hewitt. I'll ask you, did you ever attend a school at the Briehl farm near Kingston, New York?

RADER: Emphatically not, sir.

HOUSTON: Other than "not," would you mind using the word "no"?

RADER: No.

HOUSTON: You did not?

RADER: I did not.

HOUSTON: I'll ask you if you attended a Communist Party school anywhere in the year 1930—summer of 1938 or the summer of 1939?

RADER: No.

HOUSTON: Where were you in the summer of 1938?

RADER: I'll try to answer that as fully as I can. (*He begins looking at some notes that he has taken from his pocket.*) In the academic year 1937–1938 I taught at the University of Washington until the termination of the school term. As I remember, I taught in the summer school at the University of Washington in Seattle, until about August 1st. And shortly thereafter, I went with my family to stay at Canyon Creek Lodge for a vacation, for a period of approximately a month and a half.

HOUSTON: Six weeks.

RADER: Approximately a month and a half at Canyon Creek Lodge.

HOUSTON: Where is that? What state? What location?

RADER: It's in the state of Washington near Granite Falls, not very far from here, sir. I think that the woman who was operating the lodge at that time was named Mrs. Mueller, if my memory serves me correctly. Upon returning to my home in Seattle, I . . . I stayed very close to the radio for some period of time because this was the period of the Munich crisis, a very critical period in world history. And I remember—

HOUSTON: —Now, Doctor, let's get to the point—

RADER: Well, sir, I . . . I stayed in Seattle; I listened to these things very closely. If I was out of Seattle during that month, I'm very, very sure it was for a very, very short time, indeed. I am absolutely certain it was not in the state of New York. I'm absolutely certain it was not at any great distance from Seattle.

HOUSTON: You were just resting that month.

RADER: Well, uh . . . schools—the regular term of school—and I teach at the university, so I was—

HOUSTON: —Well, when did you start teaching?

RADER: Well, I wa—I was about to answer, sir. The regular term starts about the first of October, ordinarily. I'm very serious about my academic duties; I don't shirk them. I think I was in Seattle in this period and I'm absolutely certain I was not in New York in this period.

HOUSTON: All right. Now what about '39?

CANWELL: May I interrupt just a moment? I wonder if you wouldn't be just as competent to answer those questions without referring to those notes.

RADER: Well, sir, I could certainly make the attempt. I'm afraid if I did I might not be as accurate and I would like to be accurate—

CANWELL: —Well, be as accurate as you can—

RADER: —particularly when my honor is at stake and particularly when, after all, there . . . there is a question, a very serious question, raised at this hearing about my behavior, about my reputation. You're asking about nine—the summer of 1939, are you not?

HOUSTON: Yes, that's what we started out on. I may have been thrown off on some of these curves—

CANWELL: —I would like to ask you to make it as brief as you can consistently do. We have a good deal of business that is still up here.

RADER: Yes, surely. I will be as brief as I can be and be fair to myself, sir.

CANWELL: Proceed.

RADER: Well—now I believe I remained in Seattle or the near vicinity until the outbreak of the war. I am absolutely certain that in this period I was not in New York City or New York State.

HOUSTON: Now, Professor, according to your testimony, there was a six-week period after the first session of summer school in 1938 when you were unemployed and out of the city of Seattle, allegedly being at this Canyon Creek Lodge.

RADER: But not allegedly, sir, I feel quite confident about it.

HOUSTON: No, I said allegedly; I didn't say positively. I hope that I will be able to say positively too. There was a six weeks' gap there now that you were—during that period of time you could have been in New York, could you not?

RADER: No, sir.

HOUSTON: Well, if you wanted to go to New York instead of Canyon Creek Lodge, you could have been there, couldn't you?

RADER: No, sir, I did not want to go to New York instead of Canyon Creek Lodge. I was not in New York. There are people who know where I was.

HOUSTON: I didn't say, now, that you were in New York instead of Canyon Creek Lodge, but had you wanted to go, there were six weeks you could have gone, Doctor.

CANWELL: I think that is obvious on the face of the thing. I can see that—

HOUSTON: Now, there was also a six-week period in 1939 that you were not teaching, you were just around Seattle, you could have been unemployed then.

RADER: Sir, I—now wait a minute. I am very certain that if time is given, it will be possible to secure complete evidence that what I have said in all essential details is substantially correct and that I was not in New York or New York State in this period and I can tell you some ways in which I can—

HOUSTON: We—we're going to do that. I'm trying to get some ways now if I can get rid of your speeches and get a little information.

RADER: Well, I'm trying to answer your question.

HOUSTON: Now, Mr. Rader, I just want to repeat the question because it is tremendously serious. Are you or have you ever been a member of the Communist Party and can you answer it just "yes" or "no," without speeches?

RADER: No.

HOUSTON: Thank you. Do you believe in the form of government that exists in the United States of America, Dr. Winther—I mean Dr. Rader?

RADER: I certainly believe, sir, in the Constitution of the United States and the Bill of Rights and the government set up under that Constitution, as it would be interpreted, for example, by the Supreme Court.

HOUSTON: Would you change our system of society?

RADER: One thing I would be thoroughly for and anxious to do, and I think it's very, very needful, and that is to change our system of society, and particularly in the city of Seattle at the present time, in the direction of a more complete obedience in spirit and letter to the Bill of Rights.

(*Applause and cheering from some of the audience.*)

HOUSTON: Doctor, do you refer to the interpretation of the Bill of Rights by the Supreme Court of the United States—

CANWELL: I wonder, Mr. Houston, how long you expect this to go on?

HOUSTON: I'm presently through. I'm very weary. I'll just ask you one thing further. Would you be willing to work with our investigators, Doctor, in definitely and positively ascertaining with evidence, of documentary evidence, where you were in 1938 and '39, which you don't remember.

RADER: Mr. Houston, I would be very glad to work with the prosecuting attorney of King County or any of the deputies or governmental officials of the State of Washington that my counsel would approve. I follow the advice of my counsel. I think he will admit that.

HOUSTON: I've concluded with the witness. I—I think there has been a lot of speeches and statements.

CANWELL: I don't think we will care to debate it here further. I don't think we will carry this discussion any further. Now, if you are through with the witness, Mr. Houston, and you may step aside. You may be excused, I believe. You may be excused.

HOUSTON: Mr. Chairman, I believe that I have concluded with the witnesses and suggest that the hearing be concluded and that the witnesses now under subpoena be released from subpoena until called at a future date with a new subpoena—resubpoena.

CANWELL: We will now adjourn, subject to a recall of this committee, and if necessary a reissuance of some subpoenas at a later date, but all persons presently under subpoena by this committee are dismissed from that subpoena.

(*End of hearing*)

[LIGHTS FADE]

SUPERTITLE:

THEATRE OF RECORD

Canwell's Regret

1990s

CANWELL: I had a little problem with the chief investigator. I felt he did a very inept job. Houston. Anyway, that was my feeling, that he was in over his depth there. I took care of it by removing him.

[BLACKOUT]

SUPERTITLE:

THEATRE OF CONJECTURE

Fisticuffs

July 24, 1948

CANWELL, HOUSTON, *and* NIENDORFF *come downstage as the hearing room darkens.*

CANWELL: What the hell were you thinking?! You quit! You didn't go in for the kill! You ended the hearings—

NIENDORFF: —Calm down, Al, calm *down*—

CANWELL: —He pissed away the hearings—

HOUSTON: —You ended them! I merely suggested—

CANWELL: —I was going to contradict—?

HOUSTON: —I was deadlocked with Rader—

CANWELL: —He whipped your ass! I thought you were tough—

HOUSTON: —I can kick *your* ass, buddy—

(HOUSTON *takes a swing, misses;* CANWELL *connects but falls down; they scuffle.*)

NIENDORFF: —Men, men, don't—don't do this—

HOUSTON: —Nobody insults me—

CANWELL: —You let Rader get away—

HOUSTON: He's innocent! Couldn't you see? That guy is no more a Communist than—

CANWELL: —He *is* a Communist! He is a Communist until I say he isn't, is that clear?! You don't know anything about what makes a Communist. You are a blunt instrument, that's all. I needed a scalpel. I needed finesse.

HOUSTON: You decide who is and who isn't a Commun—

NIENDORFF: —You both need to calm down. We are on the same

side—they are going to file perjury charges!

CANWELL: You disappoint me, Bill.

HOUSTON: I disappoint you.

CANWELL: He was in the palm of our hand. You let Hewitt shake you—is he out of town?

NIENDORFF: He's on the train. I told the other reporters I thought he went to the airport—did you hear me? Perjury—

CANWELL: I think you should get out of town too, Bill.

HOUSTON: You firing me?

CANWELL: No, no. A vacation. Too many loose cannons around here. Go on a vacation. We'll finish up the detail stuff without you—they can file all the perjury charges they want to. Hewitt is no longer here—

NIENDORFF: —Ever hear of extradition?

CANWELL: We simply have to build a case against Rader behind the scenes.

HOUSTON: Are you crazy? He is innocent—you can't pull this off.

CANWELL: Watch me.

[LIGHTS OUT]

SUPERTITLE:

THEATRE OF RECORD

Albert Canwell

1994

CANWELL: I obtained recording equipment and one way or another could always get the wire and tape I needed to make surreptitious recordings. Quite often we merely planted a bug and listened directly so that we knew what their conversations were and who was coming and going. Much of that was done

not for permanent record. It was done just as a matter of sur-
veillance. Anyway, I did a certain amount of that.

[BLACKOUT]

SUPERTITLE:

THEATRE OF CONJECTURE

The Case of the Missing Case

1948

RADER *on phone, a bookcase behind. The top shelf is not quite full
of books.*

RADER: The scrapbook. It's not there. I've looked. Did you move
it? No. I haven't touched it. Someone must have moved it. I
asked each of the children. Yes, I know. Why? Because Hewitt
is now saying that it may have been 1940 rather than '38 or '39.
A whole other year we have to account for. I was searching—
I *have* looked in the basement. It was on the top shelf. As we
speak I'm looking at where it was. No, nothing else seems to
be missing. Nothing seems to have been jimmied. I will. I am.
I'll keep looking. Does the phone sound strange to you? No
reason. Just wondering.

[LIGHTS OUT]

SUPERTITLE:

THEATRE OF RECORD

The Parameters of Evidence

1994

CANWELL: It isn't incumbent on every investigator and every government agent to come up with documentary proof of people who are in the Communist Party. It's desirable when you can, but it's often impossible. It doesn't mean the person isn't guilty.

[BLACKOUT]

SUPERTITLE:

THEATRE OF RECORD

Hate Mail to Ted Astley

1948

TED ASTLEY *appears in light reading a letter.*

ANONYMOUS: Hello Ted. What causes you to get mixed up with the commies? You are in a hell of a fix now. Nobody loves you here. This country just isn't big enough for you and your kind. You know the true purpose of communism in this country. If you like such rotten stuff go live and stay with Uncle Joe. I'll pay your boat passage out one day if you will promise to walk the rest of the way. You should have been eager and willing to answer that you were not a commie, and glad to expose the dirty devils you know to be commies. Get out while going is good. To where your utopia is already working and save yourself the headache of rightful investigations here. From a veteran who fought to give a skunk like you and your gang American air to breathe. Wish I could turn it off for you this minute.

[BLACKOUT]

SUPERTITLE:

THEATRE OF RECORD

The Aftermath Begins

Raymond B. Allen, President, University of Washington

1949

During the following speeches, BUTTERWORTH *and* JOEY *slowly work their way back across the stage from left to right.* JOEY *is wearing an ill-fitting suit and lugging a heavy suitcase. Their progress may be wholly visible or marked with light changes. President* ALLEN *appears in light.*

ALLEN: Collusion between the university and the committee is patently ridiculous. No action will be taken by the university except through procedures laid down in existing university regulations. Complaints against six faculty members named in the hearings have been filed with the Faculty Committee on Tenure and Academic Freedom. Recommendations will be made by the Faculty Committee to the president, and by the president to the Board of Regents, which by law must make the final decision. These procedures are similar to those in effect in most universities for the protection of individual faculty members from capricious and unwarranted dismissal. Persons having tenure under the provisions of this act may be removed for one or more of the following reasons: incompetency, neglect of duty, physical or mental incapacity, dishonesty or immorality, conviction of a felony involving moral turpitude.

(*Lights out on* ALLEN *and up on* PHILLIPS.)

SUPERTITLE:

THEATRE OF RECORD
Professor Herbert J. Phillips
University of Washington Dismissal Hearings
1949

PHILLIPS: The defense of Mr. Butterworth and myself before the Board of Regents must contain certain matters. I want to argue that your obligation to protect the public interest calls for decisive discouragement of the Canwell forces. Mr. Butterworth and myself are members of the Communist Party. The program of the Party is not a secret. Any shortcomings in the extensiveness of our publicity arise from our financial limitations. The Party struggles at all times for openness. Mr. Butterworth and I see the move for our dismissal to be of a piece with the general repressive policies of a politically bankrupt capitalism.

SUPERTITLE:

THEATRE OF RECORD
Teamster President and University Regent Dave Beck
1949

BECK: We adopt the recommendations against dismissal of Jacobs, Eby, and Ethel, subject to two conditions, that these men sign affidavits that they are not now members of the Communist Party and that they be placed on probation for a period of two years. We disqualify from faculty membership Professors Phillips, Gundlach, and Butterworth.

(*Lights fade and come up on* BUTTERWORTH *and* JOEY *holding hands, being greeted by a Social Services worker,* MRS. DABNEY.)

DABNEY: You must be Joey.

BUTTERWORTH: Say hello, Joey. (*Looking at his father*) Say hello. (*Shakes his head "no"*)

DABNEY: That's all right. We'll get along just fine in no time. My name is Mrs. Dabney. Come along, young man. I'll take your bag.

(*She takes suitcase.* JOEY *is still holding his gaze on* BUTTERWORTH.)

BUTTERWORTH: You go with her. You go. Maybe just for a while. Shake hands good-bye. (BUTTERWORTH *struggling to change* JOEY*'s grip into a handshake*) Good-bye, son. I'll come see you. This is better. (*He breaks grip, turns, and goes.*)

[LIGHTS FADE QUICKLY]

SUPERTITLE:

THEATRE OF RECORD

Civil Contempt

1949

The following series of headlines are projected as a visual litany during MRS. JAMES*'s speech.*

4 WOMEN, 8 MEN ON JURY TO TRY PHILLIPS

CANWELL TESTIFIES IN PHILLIPS CASE

GUNDLACH FACES TRIAL TOMORROW

DR. PHILLIPS FREED IN CONTEMPT TRIAL

OTTENHEIMER ON TRIAL TOMORROW

ALL FACULTY AT U.W. MUST SIGN LOYALTY PLEDGE

GUNDLACH SUES DR. ALLEN

OTTENHEIMER'S GUILT WAS CLEAR, JURORS ASSERT

ALLEN GETS VFW MEDAL FOR STAND

MOTION FOR JOINT TRIAL IN JAMES CASE IS DENIED

MRS. JAMES TO GO ON TRIAL TOMORROW

JUDGE DENIES MRS. JAMES' APPEAL TO SHIFT TRIAL TO ANOTHER COUNTY

GUNDLACH'S ATTORNEYS PLAN APPEAL

JUDGE REFUSES OTTENHEIMER MISTRIAL PLEA

30 DAYS IN JAIL, $250 FINE FOR BURTON JAMES

U. OF CHICAGO TEACHERS DENY RED CHARGES

JUDGE DENIES MOTION TO DISMISS JAMES CASE

U. OF N.C. SAYS COMMUNISTS ON STAFF MUST GO

OTTENHEIMER SENTENCED TO 30 DAYS AND FINE OF $250

GUNDLACH, FIRST CANWELL DEFENDANT TO BE JAILED

MRS. JAMES, GUILTY IN SECOND TRIAL, FINED $125, 30-DAY SENTENCE, SUSPENDED

As the headlines appear and disappear MRS. JAMES *speaks.*

MRS. JAMES: Your Honor, I am at this moment in a strange and terrible position. I am about to be sentenced for a crime of which I have been convicted by a criminally selected jury. I accuse the court of denying me my proper defense, refusing permission for my witnesses to appear for me. The prosecutor has been given every opportunity for his witnesses, even including the testimony from one George Hewitt, who is now under indictment, in this office, for perjury. I accuse the prosecutor of defacing and destroying evidence. Now, finally— and this is so terrible, I find it difficult to phrase the words— I accuse this court—*you,* Your Honor—of being biased and prejudiced against me, of giving every assistance within the power of your high office to the prosecution, and of being more concerned with obtaining a guilty verdict than with serving the ends of justice in this court. I feel in making this statement, I am acting not only in my best interests but in the interests of every citizen who may find himself involved in the Superior Courts of King County.

[LIGHTS FADE]

SUPERTITLE:

THEATRE OF RECORD
Report to the Legislature
1949

CANWELL *appears in light.*

CANWELL: All of the communist fronts, their sympathizers, their followers, and their dupes, as well as those in a state of mental confusion are engaging in a concerted effort to convince the people of this state that academic freedom has been imperiled by this committee's conduct. They are in effect challenging the right of the people, through their own legislature, to question their own employees. (*Pause*) Melvin Rader did not tell the truth when he testified before the committee. Professor Rader would have had every opportunity to examine and cross-examine Hewitt. Your committee enters this in its report to the legislature to contradict and refute the manufactured stories that Professor Rader was not given an opportunity to confront and question his accuser. There is no record of this in the report because events herein related took place in the committee's executive offices. This is the first time they are publicly disclosed. Professor Rader is shown to have been sponsor for, speaker for, or to have been otherwise directly associated with twelve organizations which have been officially cited as communist fronts and subversive. Your committee feels that the perjury charge filed against Mr. Hewitt was not only hasty and unwarranted but of political significance.

[BLACKOUT]

SUPERTITLE:

THEATRE OF RECORD

Extradition Hearing for George Hewitt

New York, May 12, 1949

Judge Aaron J. Levy

No Officials from the State of Washington Present

LEVY: From what has been said, I learn that in the state of Washington there is any number of trained and iron-disciplined Communists who have operated with seeming immunity. Many of them hold almost impregnable positions of confidence and trust in their communities. I am wondering, really genuinely wondering, what the civilization of that area is. There has not been made that showing which in good conscience I consider essential to warrant my sending this man to the state of Washington to eventual slaughter. If I were he, I would be very careful about my person. Moreover, I am convinced that this man committed no crime whatever; that if perjury were committed, it was committed by Melvin Rader and that he ought to be the subject of a grand jury quiz rather than this accused; that the necessary requirements permitting extradition have not been established. And therefore this writ is sustained and the prisoner is discharged.

[BLACKOUT]

SUPERTITLE:

THEATRE OF CONJECTURE

New Circumstances

Morning, Spring 1949

BUTTERWORTH's *office.* BUTTERWORTH *enters on crutches. He is slightly drunk.* MAUD BEAL *is filling boxes with his books.*

BUTTERWORTH: Morning. Out of breath. First excursion since the accident. What are you doing?

BEAL: Just thought I'd help. Since you can't do . . . this is such a sad day.

BUTTERWORTH: What are you doing with my books? I lecture in half an hour! You're destroying my library . . .

BEAL: I'm just helping. You haven't been able to—what lecture?

BUTTERWORTH: What's going on?

BEAL: Joe, I arranged for the university to supply a truck to take your things to your home. I was afraid of something like this. How could you not know?

BUTTERWORTH: Know what?

BEAL: The letters were sent a couple of weeks ago. It's been in all the papers . . .

BUTTERWORTH: Oh well. Would you believe it? I haven't gotten around to opening my mail for some time, if the truth were known . . . What is the . . . ? Have they taken away my classes?

BEAL: I think you should go home and open your mail, Joe.

BUTTERWORTH: Oh, that's all right. Tell me. Have they axed me?

BEAL: I really don't think I should be the one to—

BUTTERWORTH: I'd rather it be you. *You* tell me. Please.

BEAL: How could you not know?

BUTTERWORTH: It's all too easy not to know certain things. Just tell me. I'm . . . let go?

BEAL: The Faculty Senate voted to not fire anyone but the Regents overrode them. You, Gundlach, and Phillips were fired outright. Eby, Ethel, and Jacobs were reprimanded and put on probation. Of course, Ted Astley was fired last fall.

BUTTERWORTH: Effective immediately?

BEAL: Yes. That was two weeks ago. It must all be in the mail. It made headlines. How could you . . .? (BUTTERWORTH *shrugs.*) I'm so sorry, Joe.

BUTTERWORTH: What about you?

BEAL: Melvin Rader and I got off scot free. So did a few others.

BUTTERWORTH (*awkwardly putting his crutches down, sitting on a box of books*): This is simply a contraction. A predictable reaction of the capitalist forces when challenged. That's all. A part of history. (*Pause*) The worst of it, I suppose, is giving up the boy. I don't think I could have handled him in the best of . . . (*He trails off for a moment.*) When I was a boy, I once stole, over a period of time, some petty cash from a neighbor. It was the money he got for selling cream from his cows. He kept it in a jar in his pantry. He had bad arthritis so I would help him occasionally. After helping him with his chores, I would pretend to use the bathroom but instead I would deplete the jar just a little bit at a time, hoping the missing cash would go unnoticed. Eventually he caught on. When he confronted me, I confessed. He did a curious thing. He told me to go home and tell my Dad and bring him back with me so we could figure out what to do about it. He was entrusting me again. I went home but I couldn't bring myself to tell my Dad. I waited, guilty and cowering, until days later, the old neighbor, stiff with arthritis, made his way over to our farm to ask my Dad why we had ignored his request and his gesture of good faith. It was the most humiliating moment of my young life. I had become paralyzed with what I later judged to be cowardice. The disappointment in those two men was . . . (*Beat*) . . . I am becoming what I was a long time ago. I can't make myself open the mail. Not even the electric bill . . . (*He stands back up.*) Maybe it's only a temporary setback.

BEAL: Let me help you. (*She does.*)

BUTTERWORTH: There are 2000 members of the Modern Language Association; surely there is an opening somewhere. I'll write them. These are simply new circumstances. One needs to adjust. Maybe I can teach elsewhere. I wonder if I'll get my pension.

BEAL: Read the letter.

BUTTERWORTH: That means no. Where will I put all these books? My apartment is small. Oh well. Some solution will present itself. If you'll excuse me. (*He starts to go.*) This is my first outing since the accident. By the time I hobble over to the Blue Moon Tavern, they should be serving. Want to join me? The books can wait.

[LIGHTS FADE]

SUPERTITLE:

THEATRE OF RECORD

Ashes to Ashes

The Canwell Living Room, Spokane, Washington

1949

CANWELL *kneels before a suggestion of a fireplace, stacks of documents beside him. He methodically feeds them, page by page, to a fire. There is an easy chair to the side. Only the scratchy sound of the following testimony is heard as a low-quality, vintage recording.*

VOICE (*voiceover*): Do you feel the legislature set you up in business to the tune of $158,000 for your own personal use?

CANWELL: No, sir.

VOICE: Why, then, did you destroy the records?

CANWELL: To protect my sources of information and to prevent them from falling into the wrong hands.

VOICE: How did you go about destroying them?

CANWELL: Much of the reports went through the fireplace of my home. Nobody said how long we should keep them. They were for our own use.

VOICE: Did you set yourself up as the sole judge of what was to be done with the records?

CANWELL: Precisely, yes, sir. I was discharging a high responsibility, and there are people in this legislature who should appreciate that I destroyed these records.

VOICE: You have previously stated that some of these records were microfilmed. Where is the microfilm?

CANWELL: I decline to answer.

VOICE: Did you give it to the FBI?

CANWELL: I decline to answer.

VOICE: Are you asking for immunity under the Fifth Amendment?

CANWELL: No. Only Communists do that.

VOICE: Do you wish to be in contempt of the legislature?

CANWELL: I am not in contempt of the legislature.

(*The action continues as:*)

SUPERTITLE:
Canwell Was Not Cited for Contempt, nor Was He Prosecuted under Section 2347 of the Criminal Code for Injury or Destruction of Public Records

SUPERTITLE:
THEATRE OF CONJECTURE

Supertitle fades as CANWELL'S *wife,* MARSINAH, *enters and sits in the easy chair. She looks straight ahead. There is a formality about the following:*

CANWELL: Losing the election may be a blessing in disguise. I might be more effective behind the scenes, out of the public glare. There is plenty of work still to do. Intriguing stuff. A federal agent has been slipping me interesting information—wants to hear what I find out. Some East Coast couple has bought a ranch in the Okanogan. She's a New Dealer—worked for the Roosevelt administration. The question is, why would anyone not from this area set themselves up in that godforsaken country? They have built an airstrip on the place and it is arousing curiosity among the people in the surrounding . . . planes coming in and going out . . . I think they're Jews. Goldmark. I will just keep doing what I do in a quieter way. You all right? (MARSINAH *turns to look at him, implacably.*) You are the most stunning woman I've ever set eyes on.

MARSINAH: All this and flattery too?

[LIGHTS FADE]

SUPERTITLE:

THEATRE OF RECORD

Elegies

As the following speeches are heard, BUTTERWORTH, *toward the end of his life, ragged and dirty, is slowly staggering home from the Blue Moon Tavern. He is so drunk, staying upright requires all his concentration. His progress at one point is interrupted by a deep coughing fit.* CAUGHLAN *appears in light.*

CAUGHLAN: Any society discourages criticism of its underlying assumptions.

(*Light out and up on:*)

PHILLIPS: John Adams, second president of the United States, once said, "Remember, democracy never lasts long. It soon wastes, exhausts and murders itself. There never was a democracy that didn't commit suicide."

(*Light out and up on:*)

MRS. JAMES: Our building still stands at the corner of 41st and University Way and is being successfully used by the Drama Department of the University of Washington by a generation of students who have never heard of us or the hearings or the trials. The elm tree we planted still shades the theatre.

(*Light out and up on:*)

PHILLIPS: I think all this might fall under the category of a . . . giant . . . *misunderstanding.*

(*Lights fade on* PHILLIPS.)

(BUTTERWORTH *crossing the stage, stops, turns upstage, shaky as a man in a rowboat, unzips, and begins to urinate as:*)

[LIGHTS FADE]

[END OF PLAY]

Sources and Further Reading

Albert F. Canwell: An Oral History. Washington State Oral History Program. Olympia: Office of the Secretary of State, 1997.

Alinsky, Saul D. *Rules for Radicals.* New York: Vintage Books, 1972.

Astley, Theodore. Interview by playwright. Videotaped. Seattle, 1995.

————. Personal papers and letters.

Canwell, Albert F. Interview by playwright. Videotaped. Spokane, 1993.

Canwell, Albert F., and Committee Members. "Report of the Joint Legislative Fact-Finding Committee on Un-American Activities." Typescript. Olympia, Wash., 1949.

Caughlan, John. Interview by playwright. Videotaped. Seattle, 1993.

Countryman, Vern. *Un-American Activities in the State of Washington: The Work of the Canwell Committee.* Ithaca: Cornell University Press, 1951.

Crossman, Richard, ed. *The God That Failed.* New York: Bantam Books, 1965.

Dennis, Peggy. *The Autobiography of an American Communist.* Berkeley and Westport: Creative Arts Book Co., 1997.

Dwyer, William L. *The Goldmark Case: An American Libel Trial.* Seattle: University of Washington Press, 1984.

Eby, Harold. Interview by playwright. Audiotaped. 1993.

Gornick, Vivian. *The Romance of American Communism.* New York: Basic Books, 1977.

James, Florence Bean. "Fist upon a Star." Unpublished autobiography. Playwright's archives.

Joint Legislative Fact-Finding Committee on Un-American Activities. *Un-American Activities in Washington State: First and Second Reports to the 31st Washington Legislature.* Olympia, 1948–49.

Marx, Karl, and Engels, Friedrich. *The Communist Manifesto.* New York: Viking Penguin, 1985.

Padover, Saul K., ed. *The Essential Marx.* New York: New American Library, Mentor, 1979.

Pellegrini, Virginia. Interview by playwright. Videotaped. 1994.

Phillips, Herbert J. (Scoop). Copies of personal papers and letters. Playwright's archives.

Rader, Melvin. *False Witness.* Seattle: University of Washington Press, 1979.

Sanders, Jane. *Cold War on the Campus: Academic Freedom at the University of Washington, 1946–64.* Seattle: University of Washington Press, 1979.

Seeing Red. A documentary film produced and directed by James Klein and Julia Reichert. Heartland Productions, 1984.

University of Washington. *Communism and Academic Freedom: The Record of the Tenure Case at the University of Washington.* Seattle: University of Washington Press, 1949.